Who are to be the

New Intellectuals?

"Any man or woman who is willing to think. All those who know that man's life must be guided by reason, those who value their own life and are not willing to surrender it to the cult of despair in the modern jungle of cynical impotence, just as they are not willing to surrender the world to the Dark Ages and the rule of the brutes."

This book presents the essentials of Ayn Rand's philosophy "for those who wish to acquire an integrated view of existence." In the title essay, she offers an analysis of Western culture, discusses the causes of its progress, its decline, its present bankruptcy, and points the road to an intellectual renaissance.

Ayn Rand raises the standard of "reason, individualism, and capitalism" against today's prevalent doctrines of mysticism, altruism, and collectivism. The novels that present her unconventional views have become modern classics.

FOR THE NEW INTELLECTUAL

The Philosophy of
AYN RAND

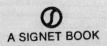

A SIGNET BOOK

SIGNET
Published by New American Library, a division of
Penguin Putnam Inc., 375 Hudson Street,
New York, New York 10014, U.S.A.
Penguin Books Ltd, 27 Wrights Lane,
London W8 5TZ, England
Penguin Books Australia Ltd, Ringwood,
Victoria, Australia
Penguin Books Canada Ltd, 10 Alcorn Avenue,
Toronto, Ontario, Canada M4V 3B2
Penguin Books (N.Z.) Ltd, 182–190 Wairau Road,
Auckland 10, New Zealand

Penguin Books Ltd, Registered Offices:
Harmondsworth, Middlesex, England

Published by Signet, an imprint of New American Library,
a division of Penguin Putnam Inc.
40 39 38 37 36 35 34

Information about other books by Ayn Rand and her philosophy, Objectivism, may be obtained by writing to OBJECTIVISM, Box 177, Murray Hill Station, New York, New York, 10157 USA.

 REGISTERED TRADEMARK—MARCA REGISTRADA

Printed in the United States of America

CONTENTS

Preface

This book is intended for those who wish to assume the responsibility of becoming the new intellectuals. It contains the main philosophical passages from my novels and presents the outline of a new philosophical system.

The full system is implicit in these excerpts (particularly in Galt's speech), but its fundamentals are indicated only in the widest terms and require a detailed, systematic presentation in a philosophical treatise. I am working on such a treatise at present; it will deal predominantly with the issue which is barely touched upon in Galt's speech: epistemology, and will present a new theory of the nature, source and validation of concepts. This work will require several years; until then, I offer the present book as a lead or a summary for those who wish to acquire an integrated view of existence. They may regard it as a basic outline; it will give them the guidance they need, but only if they think through and understand the exact meaning and the full implications of these excerpts.

I am often asked whether I am primarily a novelist or a philosopher. The answer is: both. In a certain sense, every novelist is a philosopher, because one cannot present a picture of human existence without a philosophical framework; the novelist's only choice is whether that framework is present in his story explicitly or implicitly, whether he is aware of it or not, whether he holds his philosophical convictions consciously or subconsciously. This involves another choice: whether his work is his individual projection of existing philosophical ideas or whether he originates a philosophical framework of his own. I did the second. That is not the specific task of a novelist; I had to do it, because my basic view of

vii

man and of existence was in conflict with most of the existing philosophical theories. In order to define, explain and present my concept of man, I had to become a philosopher in the specific meaning of the term.

For those who may be interested in the chronological development of my thinking, I have included excerpts from all four of my novels. They may observe the progression from a political theme in *We the Living* to a metaphysical theme in *Atlas Shrugged*.

These excerpts are necessarily condensed summaries, because the full statement of the subjects involved is presented, in each novel, by means of the events of the story. The events are the concretes and the particulars, of which the speeches are the abstract summations.

When I say that these excerpts are merely an outline, I do not mean to imply that my full system is still to be defined or discovered; I had to define it before I could start writing *Atlas Shrugged*. Galt's speech is its briefest summary.

Until I complete the presentation of my philosophy in a fully detailed form, this present book may serve as an outline or a program or a manifesto.

For reasons which are made clear in the following pages, the name I have chosen for my philosophy is *Objectivism*.

AYN RAND

October, 1960

For the

New Intellectual

When a man, a business corporation or an entire society is approaching bankruptcy, there are two courses that those involved can follow: they can evade the reality of their situation and act on a frantic, blind, range-of-the-moment expediency—not daring to look ahead, wishing no one would name the truth, yet desperately hoping that something will save them somehow—or they can identify the situation, check their premises, discover their hidden assets and start rebuilding.

America, at present, is following the first course. The grayness, the stale cynicism, the noncommittal cautiousness, the guilty evasiveness of our public voices suggest the attitude of the courtiers in the story "The Emperor's New Clothes" who professed admiration for the Emperor's non-existent garments, having accepted the assertion that anyone who failed to perceive them was morally depraved at heart.

Let me be the child in the story and declare that the Emperor is naked—or that America is culturally bankrupt.

In any given period of history, a culture is to be judged by its dominant philosophy, by the prevalent trend of its intellectual life as expressed in morality, in politics, in economics, in art. Professional intellectuals are the voice of a culture and are, therefore, its leaders, its integrators and its bodyguards. America's intellectual leadership has collapsed. Her virtues, her values, her enormous power are scattered in a silent underground and will remain private, subjective, historically impotent if left without intellectual expression. America is a country without voice or defense—a country sold out and abandoned by her intellectual bodyguards.

Bankruptcy is defined as the state of being at the end of one's resources. What are the intellectual values or resources offered to us by the present guardians of our culture? In philosophy, we are taught that man's mind is impotent, that reality is unknowable, that knowledge is an illusion, and reason a superstition. In psychology, we are told that man is a helpless automaton, determined by forces beyond his control, motivated by innate depravity. In literature, we are shown a line-up of murderers, dipsomaniacs, drug addicts, neurotics and psychotics as representatives of man's soul—and are invited to identify our own among them—with the belligerent assertions that life is a sewer, a foxhole or a rat race, with the whining injunctions that we must love everything, except virtue, and forgive everything, except greatness. In politics, we are told that America, the greatest, noblest, freest country on earth, is politically and morally inferior to Soviet Russia, the bloodiest dictatorship in history—and that our wealth should be given away to the savages of Asia and Africa, with apologies for the fact that we have produced it while they haven't. If we look at modern intellectuals, we are confronted with the grotesque spectacle of such characteristics as militant uncertainty, crusading cynicism, dogmatic agnosticism, boastful self-abasement and self-righteous depravity—in an atmosphere of guilt, of panic, of despair, of boredom and of all-pervasive evasion. If this is not the state of being at the end of one's resources, there is no further place to go.

Everybody seems to agree that civilization is facing a crisis, but nobody cares to define its nature, to discover its cause and to assume the responsibility of formulating a solution. In times of danger, a morally healthy culture rallies its values, its self-esteem and its crusading spirit to fight for its moral ideals with full, righteous confidence. But this is not what we see today. If we ask our intellectual leaders what *are* the ideals we should fight for, their answer is such a sticky puddle of stale syrup—of benevolent bromides and apologetic generalities about brother love, global progress and universal prosperity at America's expense—that a fly would not die *for* it or *in* it.

One of America's tragic errors is that too many of her best minds believe—as they did in the past—that the solution is to turn anti-intellectual and rely on some cracker-barrel sort of folksy wisdom. The exact opposite is true. What we need most urgently is to recognize the enormous power and the crucial importance of the intellectual professions. A culture cannot exist without a constant stream of ideas and the alert, independent minds who originate them; it cannot exist without a philosophy of life, without those who formulate it and express it. A country without intellectuals is like a body without a head. And *that* is precisely the position of America today. Our present state of cultural disintegration is not maintained and prolonged by intellectuals as such, but by the fact that we haven't any. The majority of those who posture as intellectuals today are frightened zombies, posturing in a vacuum of their own making, who admit their abdication from the realm of the intellect by embracing such doctrines as Existentialism and Zen Buddhism.

After decades of preaching that the hallmark of an intellectual consists of proclaiming the impotence of the intellect, these modern zombies are left aghast before the fact that they have succeeded—that they are impotent to ignite the lights of civilization, which *they* have extinguished—that they are impotent to halt the triumphant advance of the primordial brute, whom *they* have released—that they have no answer to give to those voices out of the Dark Ages who gloat that *reason* and *freedom* have had their chance and have failed, and that the future, like the long night of the past, belongs once more to *faith* and *force*.

If all the manufacturers of railroad engines suddenly went irrational and began to manufacture covered wagons instead, nobody would accept the claim that this is a progressive innovation or that the iron horse has failed; and many men would step into the industrial vacuum to start manufacturing railroad engines. But when this happens in philosophy—when we are offered Zen Buddhism and its equivalents as the latest word in human thought—nobody, so far, has chosen to step into the intellectual vacuum to carry on the work of man's mind.

Thus our great industrial civilization is now expected to run railroads, airlines, intercontinental missiles and H-bomb stock piles by the guidance of philosophical doctrines created by and for barefoot savages who lived in mudholes, scratched the soil for a handful of grain and gave thanks to the statues of distorted animals whom they worshipped as superior to man.

Historically, the professional intellectual is a very recent phenomenon: he dates only from the industrial revolution. There are no professional intellectuals in primitive, savage societies, there are only witch doctors. There were no professional intellectuals in the Middle Ages, there were only monks in monasteries. In the post-Renaissance era, prior to the birth of capitalism, the men of the intellect—the philosophers, the teachers, the writers, the early scientists—were men without a profession, that is: without a socially recognized position, without a market, without a means of earning a livelihood. Intellectual pursuits had to depend on the accident of inherited wealth or on the favor and financial support of some wealthy protector. And wealth was not earned on an open market, either; wealth was acquired by conquest, by force, by political power, or by the favor of those who held political power. Tradesmen were more vulnerably and precariously dependent on favor than the intellectuals.

The professional businessman and the professional intellectual came into existence together, as brothers born of the industrial revolution. Both are the sons of capitalism—and if they perish, they will perish together. The tragic irony will be that they will have destroyed each other; and the major share of the guilt will belong to the intellectual.

With very rare and brief exceptions, pre-capitalist societies had no place for the creative power of man's mind, neither in the creation of ideas nor in the creation of wealth. Reason and its practical expression—free trade—were forbidden as a sin and a crime, or were tolerated, usually as ignoble activities, under the control of authorities who could revoke the tolerance at whim. Such societies were ruled by faith and its practical expression: force. There were no makers of knowledge and no makers of wealth; there were only witch doctors and tribal chiefs. These two figures dominate every anti-rational period of history, whether one calls them tribal chief and witch doctor—or absolute monarch and religious leader—or dictator and logical positivist.

"The tragic joke of human history"—I am quoting John Galt in *Atlas Shrugged*—"is that on any of the altars men erected, it was always man whom they immolated and the animal whom they enshrined. It was always the animal's attributes, not man's, that humanity worshipped: the idol of instinct and the idol of force—the mystics and the kings—the mystics, who longed for an irresponsible consciousness and ruled by means of the claim that their dark emotions were superior to reason, that knowledge came in blind, causeless fits, blindly to be followed, not doubted—and the kings, who ruled by means of claws and muscles, with conquest as their method and looting as their aim, with a club or a gun as sole sanction of their power. The defenders of man's soul were concerned with his feelings, and the defenders of man's body were concerned with his stomach—but both were united against his mind."

These two figures—the man of faith and the man of force—are philosophical archetypes, psychological symbols and historical reality. As philosophical archetypes, they embody two variants of a certain view of man and of existence. As psychological symbols, they represent the basic motivation of a great many men who exist in any era, culture or society. As historical reality, they are the actual rulers of most of mankind's societies, who rise to power whenever men abandon reason.*

The essential characteristics of these two remain the same in all ages: *Attila*, the man who rules by brute force, acts on the range of the moment, is concerned with nothing but the physical reality immediately before him, respects nothing but man's muscles, and regards a fist, a club or a gun as the only answer to any problem—and *the Witch Doctor*, the man who dreads physical reality, dreads the necessity of practical action, and escapes into his emotions, into visions of some mystic realm where his wishes enjoy a supernatural power unlimited by the absolute of nature.

Superficially, these two may appear to be opposites, but observe what they have in common: a consciousness held down to the *perceptual* method of functioning, an awareness that does not choose to extend beyond the automatic, the immediate, the given, the involuntary, which means: an animal's "epistemology" or as near to it as a human consciousness can come.

Man's consciousness shares with animals the first two stages of its development: sensations and perceptions; but it is the third state, *conceptions*, that makes him man. Sensations are integrated into perceptions automatically, by the brain of a man or of an animal. But to integrate perceptions into conceptions by a process of abstraction, is a feat that man alone has the power to perform—and he has to perform it *by choice*. The process of abstraction, and of concept-forma-

---

* I am indebted to Nathaniel Branden for many valuable observations on this subject and for his eloquent designation of the two archetypes, which I shall use hereafter: *Attila and the Witch Doctor*.

tion is a process of reason, of *thought*; it is not automatic nor instinctive nor involuntary nor infallible. Man has to initiate it, to sustain it and to bear responsibility for its results. The pre-conceptual level of consciousness is nonvolitional; volition begins with the first syllogism. Man has the choice to think or to evade—to maintain a state of full awareness or to drift from moment to moment, in a semi-conscious daze, at the mercy of whatever associational whims the unfocused mechanism of his consciousness produces.

But the living organisms that possess the faculty of consciousness need to exercise it in order to survive. An animal's consciousness functions automatically; an animal perceives what it is able to perceive and survives accordingly, no further than the perceptual level permits and no better. Man cannot survive on the perceptual level of *his* consciousness; his senses do not provide him with an automatic guidance, they do not give him the knowledge he needs, only the *material* of knowledge, which his mind has to integrate. Man is the only living species who has to perceive reality—which means: to be *conscious*—by choice. But he shares with other species the penalty of unconsciousness: destruction. For an animal, the question of survival is primarily physical; for man, primarily epistemological.

Man's unique reward, however, is that while animals survive by adjusting themselves to their background, man survives by adjusting his background to himself. If a drought strikes them, animals perish—man builds irrigation canals; if a flood strikes them, animals perish—man builds dams; if a carnivorous pack attacks them animals perish—man writes the Constitution of the United States. But one does not obtain food, safety or freedom—by instinct.

It is against this faculty, the faculty of *reason*, that Attila and the Witch Doctor rebel. The key to both their souls is their longing for the effortless, irresponsible, automatic consciousness of an animal. Both dread the necessity, the risk and the responsibility of rational cognition. Both dread the fact that "nature, to be commanded, must be obeyed." Both seek to exist, not by conquering nature, but by adjusting to the given, the immediate, the known. There is only one means of survival for those who do not choose to conquer nature: to conquer those who do.

The *physical* conquest of men is Attila's method of survival. He regards men as others regard fruit trees or farm animals:

as objects in nature, his for the seizing. But while a good
farmer knows, at least, that fruit trees and animals have a
specific nature and require a specific kind of handling, the
perceptual mentality of Attila does not extend to so abstract a
level: men, to him, are a natural phenomenon and an irreducible primary, as all natural phenomena are irreducible primaries
to an animal. Attila feels no need to understand, to explain,
nor even to wonder, *how* men manage to produce the things he
covets—*"somehow"* is a fully satisfactory answer inside his
skull, which refuses to consider such questions as "how?" and
"why?" or such concepts as identity and causality. All he
needs, his "urges" tell him, is bigger muscles, bigger clubs or a
bigger gang than theirs in order to seize their bodies and their
products, after which their bodies will obey his commands and
will provide him, somehow, with the satisfaction of any whim.
He approaches men as a beast of prey, and the consequences
of his actions or the possibility of exhausting his victims never
enters his consciousness, which does not choose to extend
beyond the given moment. His view of the universe does not
include the power of production. The power of destruction, of
brute force, is, to him, metaphysically omnipotent.

An Attila never thinks of creating, only of *taking over.*
Whether he conquers a neighboring tribe or overruns a continent, material looting is his only goal and it ends with the act
of seizure: he has no other purpose, no plan, no system to
impose on the conquered, no values. His pleasures are closer
to the level of sensations than of perceptions: food, drink,
palatial shelter, rich clothing, indiscriminate sex, contests of
physical prowess, gambling—all those activities which do not
demand or involve the use of the conceptual level of consciousness. He does not originate his pleasures: he desires
and pursues whatever those around him seem to find desirable.
Even in the realm of desires, he does not create, he merely
takes over.

But a human being cannot live his life moment by moment;
a human consciousness preserves a certain continuity and demands a certain degree of integration, whether a man seeks it
or not. A human being needs a frame of reference, a compre-
hensive view of existence, no matter how rudimentary, and,
since his consciousness *is* volitional, a sense of being *right,*
a moral justification of his actions, which means: a philosophical code of values. Who, then, provides Attila with
values? The Witch Doctor.

If Attila's method of survival is the conquest of those who conquer nature, the Witch Doctor's method of survival is safer, he believes, and spares him the risks of physical conflict. *His* method is the conquest of those who conquer those who conquer nature. It is not men's bodies that he seeks to rule, but men's souls.

To Attila, as to an animal, the phenomena of nature are an irreducible primary. To the Witch Doctor, as to an animal, the irreducible primary is the automatic phenomena of his own consciousness.

An animal has no critical faculty; he has no control over the function of his brain and no power to question its content. To an animal, whatever strikes his awareness is an absolute that corresponds to reality—or rather, it is a distinction he is incapable of making: reality, to him, is whatever he senses or feels. And *this* is the Witch Doctor's epistemological ideal, the mode of consciousness he strives to induce in himself. To the Witch Doctor, emotions are tools of cognition, and wishes take precedence over facts. He seeks to escape the risks of a quest for knowledge by obliterating the distinction between consciousness and reality, between the perceiver and the perceived, hoping that an automatic certainty and an infallible knowledge of the universe will be granted to him by the blind, unfocused stare of his eyes turned inward, contemplating the sensations, the feelings, the urgings, the muggy associational twistings projected by the rudderless mechanism of his undirected consciousness. Whatever his mechanism produces is an absolute not to be questioned; and whenever it clashes with reality, it is reality that he ignores.

Since the clash is constant, the Witch Doctor's solution is to believe that what he perceives is another, "higher" reality —where his wishes are omnipotent, where contradictions are possible and A is non-A, where his assertions, which are false on earth, become true and acquire the status of a "superior" truth which *he* perceives by means of a special faculty denied to other, "inferior," beings. The only validation of his consciousness he can obtain on earth is the belief and the obedience of others, when they accept his "truth" as superior to their own perception of reality. While Attila extorts their obedience by means of a club, the Witch Doctor obtains it by means of a much more powerful weapon: he pre-empts the field of *morality*.

There is no way to turn morality into a weapon of enslavement except by divorcing it from man's reason and from the goals of his own existence. There is no way to degrade man's life on earth except by the lethal opposition of the *moral* and the *practical*. Morality is a code of values to guide man's choices and actions; when it is set to oppose his own life and mind, it makes him turn against himself and blindly act as the tool of his own destruction. There is no way to make a human being accept the role of a sacrificial animal except by destroying his self-esteem. There is no way to destroy his self-esteem except by making him reject his own consciousness. There is no way to make him reject his own consciousness except by convincing him of its impotence.

The damnation of this earth as a realm where nothing is possible to man but pain, disaster and defeat, a realm inferior to another, "higher," reality; the damnation of all values, enjoyment, achievement and success on earth as a proof of depravity; the damnation of man's mind as a source of *pride*, and the damnation of reason as a "limited," deceptive, unreliable, impotent faculty, incapable of perceiving the "real" reality and the "true" truth; the split of man in two, setting his consciousness (his soul) against his body, and his moral values against his own interest; the damnation of man's nature, body and *self* as evil; the commandment of self-sacrifice, renunciation, suffering, obedience, humility and faith, as the good; the damnation of life and the worship of death, with the promise of rewards beyond the grave—*these* are the necessary tenets of the Witch Doctor's view of existence, as they have been in every variant of Witch Doctor philosophy throughout the course of mankind's history.

The secret of the Witch Doctor's power lies in the fact that man needs an integrated view of life, a *philosophy*, whether he is aware of his need or not—and whenever, through ignorance, cowardice or mental sloth, men choose not to be aware of it, their chronic sense of guilt, uncertainty and terror makes them feel that the Witch Doctor's philosophy is true.

The first to feel it is Attila.

The man who lives by brute force, at the whim and mercy of the moment, lives on a narrow island suspended in a fog of the unknown, where invisible threats and unpredictable disasters can descend upon him any morning. He is willing to surrender his consciousness to the man who offers him protection against those intangible questions which he does not wish to consider, yet dreads.

Attila's fear of reality is as great as the Witch Doctor's. Both hold their consciousness on a subhuman level and method of functioning: Attila's brain is a jumble of concretes unintegrated by abstractions; the Witch Doctor's brain is a miasma of floating abstractions unrelated to concretes. Both are guided and motivated—ultimately—not by thoughts, but by feelings and whims. Both cling to their whims as to their only certainty. Both feel secretly inadequate to the task of dealing with existence.

Thus they come to need each other. Attila feels that the Witch Doctor can give him what he lacks: a long-range view, an insurance against the dark unknown of tomorrow or next week or next year, a code of moral values to sanction his actions and to disarm his victims. The Witch Doctor feels that Attila can give him the material means of survival, can protect him from physical reality, can spare him the necessity of practical action, and can enforce his mystic edicts on any recalcitrant who may choose to challenge his authority. Both of them are incomplete parts of a human being, who seek completion in each other: the man of muscle and the man of feelings, seeking to exist without *mind*.

Since no man can fully escape the conceptual level of consciousness, it is not the case that Attila and the Witch Doctor cannot or do not think; they can and do—but thinking, to them, is not a means of perceiving reality, it is a means of justifying their escape from the necessity of rational perception. Reason, to them, is a means of defeating their victims, a menial servant charged with the task of rationalizing the metaphysical validity and power of their whims. Just as a bank robber will spend years of planning, ingenuity and effort in order to prove to himself that he can exist without effort, so both Attila and the Witch Doctor will go to any length of cunning, calculation and thought in order to demonstrate the impotence of thought and preserve the image of a pliable universe where miracles are possible and whims are efficacious. The power of *ideas* has no reality for either of them, and neither cares to learn that the proof of that power lies in his own chronic sense of guilt and terror.

Thus Attila and the Witch Doctor form an alliance and divide their respective domains. Attila rules the realm of men's physical existence—the Witch Doctor rules the realm of

men's consciousness. Attila herds men into armies—the Witch
Doctor sets the armies' goals. Attila conquers empires—the
Witch Doctor writes their laws. Attila loots and plunders—the
Witch Doctor exhorts the victims to surpass their selfish concern with material property. Attila slaughters—the Witch Doctor proclaims to the survivors that scourges are a retribution
for their sins. Attila rules by means of *fear*, by keeping men
under a constant threat of destruction—the Witch Doctor
rules by means of *guilt*, by keeping men convinced of their
innate depravity, impotence and insignificance. Attila turns
men's life on earth into a living hell—the Witch Doctor tells
them that it could not be otherwise.

But the alliance of the two rulers is precarious: it is based
on mutual fear and mutual contempt. Attila is an extrovert,
resentful of any concern with consciousness—the Witch Doctor is an introvert, resentful of any concern with physical
existence. Attila professes scorn for values, ideals, principles,
theories, abstractions—the Witch Doctor professes scorn for
material property, for wealth, for man's body, for this earth.
Attila considers the Witch Doctor impractical—the Witch
Doctor considers Attila immoral. But, secretly, each of them
believes that the other possesses a mysterious faculty *he* lacks,
that the other is the true master of reality, the true exponent
of the power to deal with existence. In terms, not of thought,
but of chronic anxiety, it is the Witch Doctor who believes
that brute force rules the world—and it is Attila who believes in the supernatural; his name for it is "fate" or "luck."

Against whom is this alliance formed? Against those men
whose existence and character both Attila and the Witch
Doctor refuse to admit into their view of the universe: the
men who produce. In any age or society, there are men who
think and work, who discover how to deal with existence, how
to produce the intellectual and the material values it requires.
These are the men whose effort is the only means of survival
for the parasites of all varieties: the Attilas, the Witch Doctors
and the human ballast. The ballast consists of those who go
through life in a state of unfocused stupor, merely repeating
the words and the motions they learned from others. But
the men from whom they learn, the men who are first to
discover any scrap of new knowledge, are the men who
deal with reality, with the task of conquering nature, and
who, to that extent, assume the responsibility of cognition: of
exercising their rational faculty.

A producer is any man who works and knows what he is doing. He may function on a fully human, conceptual level of awareness only some part of his time, but, to that extent, he is the Atlas who supports the existence of mankind; he may spend the rest of his time in an unthinking daze, like the others, and, to that extent, he is the exploited, drained, tortured, self-destroying victim of their schemes.

Men's epistemology—or, more precisely, their *psycho-epistemology*, their method of awareness—is the most fundamental standard by which they can be classified. Few men are consistent in that respect; most men keep switching from one level of awareness to another, according to the circumstances or the issues involved, ranging from moments of full rationality to an almost somnambulistic stupor. But the battle of human history is fought and determined by those who are predominantly consistent, those who, for good or evil, are committed to and motivated by their chosen psycho-epistemology and its corollary view of existence—with echoes responding to them, in support or opposition, in the switching, flickering souls of the others.

A man's method of using his consciousness determines his method of survival. The three contestants are Attila, the Witch Doctor and the Producer—or the man of force, the man of feelings, the man of reason—or the brute, the mystic, the thinker. The rest of mankind calls it expedient to be tossed by the current of events from one of those roles to another, not choosing to identify the fact that those three are the source which determines the current's direction.

The producers, so far, have been the forgotten men of history. With the exception of a few brief periods, the producers have not been the leaders or the term-setters of men's societies, although the degree of their influence and freedom was the degree of a society's welfare and progress. Most societies have been ruled by Attila and the Witch Doctor. The cause is not some innate tendency to evil in human nature, but the fact that reason is a volitional faculty which man has to choose to discover, employ and preserve. Irrationality is a state of default, the state of an unachieved human stature. When men do not choose to reach the conceptual level, their consciousness has no recourse but to its automatic, perceptual, semi-animal functions. If a missing link between the human and the animal species is to be found, Attila and the Witch Doctor are that missing link—the profiteers on men's default.

The sound of the first human step in recorded history, the prelude to the entrance of the producer on the historical scene, was the birth of philosophy in ancient Greece. All earlier cultures had been ruled, not by reason, but by mysticism: the task of philosophy—the formulation of an integrated view of man, of existence, of the universe—was the monopoly of various religions that enforced their views by the authority of a claim to supernatural knowledge and dictated the rules that controlled men's lives. Philosophy was born in a period when Attila was impotent to assist the Witch Doctor—when a comparative degree of political freedom undercut the power of mysticism and, for the first time, man was free to face an unobstructed universe, free to declare that his *mind* was competent to deal with all the problems of his existence and that *reason* was his only means of knowledge.

Even though the influence of the Witch Doctor's views permeated the works of the early philosophers, reason, for the first time, was identified and acknowledged as man's ruling faculty, a recognition it had never been granted before. Plato's system was a monument to the Witch Doctor's metaphysics—with its two realities, with the physical world as a semi-illusory, imperfect, inferior realm, subordinated to a realm of *abstractions* (which means, in fact, though not in Plato's statement: subordinated to man's consciousness), with reason in the position of an inferior but necessary servant that paves the way for the ultimate burst of mystic revelation which discloses a "superior" truth. But Aristotle's philosophy was the intellect's Declaration of Independence. Aristotle, the father of logic, should be given the title of the world's first *intellectual*, in the purest and noblest sense of that word. No matter what remnants of Platonism did exist in Aristotle's system, his incomparable achievement lay in the fact that he defined the *basic* principles of a rational view of existence and of man's consciousness: that there is only *one* reality, the one which man perceives—that it exists as an *objective* absolute (which means: independently of the consciousness, the wishes or the feelings of any perceiver)—that the task of man's consciousness is to *perceive*, not to create, reality—that abstractions are man's method of integrating his sensory material—that man's mind is his only tool of knowledge —that A is A.

If we consider the fact that to this day everything that makes us civilized beings, every rational value that we possess—including the birth of science, the industrial revolution, the creation of the United States, even the structure of our language—is the result of Aristotle's influence, of the degree to which, explicitly or implicitly, men accepted his epistemological principles, we would have to say: never have so many owed so much to one man.

Just as the Witch Doctor is impotent without Attila, so Attila is impotent without the Witch Doctor; neither can make his power last without the other. Politically, the centuries of the Greco-Roman civilization were still dominated by Attila (by the rule of local tyrants or tribal aristocracies), but it was a tame, uncertain, subdued Attila, who had to contend with the influence of philosophy (not of faith) in men's minds. The best aspects of Western civilization still owe their roots to the intellectual achievements of that era.

Attila regained his power with the rise of *statism* in the Roman Empire. What followed was the fall of Rome, as a drained hulk, bankrupt in spirit and body, unable to muster any power of resistance to the invasion of barbarian hordes —then the looting and devastation of Europe by the literal *Attila*, and the centuries of brute violence, of bloody tribal warfare, of unrecorded chaos, known as the Dark Ages. The Witch Doctors were re-emerging, with a new version of mysticism, in answer to the pleas for help of the various local Attilas, who were bowing to them voluntarily, in speedy conversions, in exchange for the guidance of some form of basic principles to help them stabilize their power.

The Middle Ages was a period ruled by the Witch Doctor, in a firm, if mutually jealous, alliance with Attila. The Witch Doctors controlled every aspect of human life and thought, while the feudal Attilas looted one another's domains, collected material tributes from serfs—who worked, lived and starved in subhuman conditions—and maintained the Witch Doctors' monopoly on spiritual law and order, by the power to burn heretics at the stake.

Philosophy, in that era, existed as a "handmaiden of theology," and the dominant influence was, appropriately, Plato's in the form of Plotinus and Augustine. Aristotle's works were lost to the scholars of Europe for centuries. The prelude to the Renaissance was the return of Aristotle via Thomas Aquinas.

The Renaissance—the rebirth of man's mind—blasted the rule of the Witch Doctor sky-high, setting the *earth* free of his power. The liberation was not total, nor was it immediate: the convulsions lasted for centuries, but the *cultural* influence of mysticism—of avowed mysticism—was broken. Men could no longer be told to reject their mind as an impotent tool, when the proof of its potency was so magnificently evident that the lowest perceptual-level mentality was not able fully to evade it: men were seeing the achievements of *science*.

The Renaissance did not dethrone Attila at once: he clung to his fading power a while longer, building his absolute monarchies on the remnants of his crumbling feudal state. But once again, as in the Greco-Roman era, Attila was ineffectual when left on his own. He was mentally helpless and scared, unable to cope with the tide of liberation sweeping the world. He ran blindly amuck in the practice of his only skill and purpose, that of material extortion, bringing nations to ragged poverty by his constant wars and levies, taxing away the last of his subjects' possessions. But when it came to intellectual issues, he kept appeasing the advocates of freedom, he assumed the role of their pupil, protector and "patron of the arts," lapsing occasionally into frantic bursts of censorship and persecution, then returning to the role of "enlightened monarch." Attila, like any bully and like many animals, feels confident only when he smells fear in his opponents—and it is not fear that thinkers project when they fight for the freedom of the mind. "The divine right of kings" was not much of a weapon against men who were discovering the rights of *man*.

The industrial revolution completed the task of the Renaissance: it blasted Attila off his throne. For the first time in history, men gained control over physical nature and threw off the control of men over men—that is: men discovered science and political freedom.

The first society in history whose leaders were neither Attilas nor Witch Doctors, a society led, dominated and created by the *Producers,* was the United States of America. The moral code implicit in its political principles was not the Witch Doctor's code of self-sacrifice. The political principles embodied in its Constitution were not Attila's blank check on brute force, but men's protection *against* any future Attila's ambition.

The Founding Fathers were neither passive, death-worshipping mystics nor mindless, power-seeking looters; as a political group, they were a phenomenon unprecedented in history: they were *thinkers* who were also men of action. They had rejected the soul-body dichotomy, with its two corollaries: the impotence of man's mind and the damnation of this earth; they had rejected the doctrine of suffering as man's metaphysical fate, they proclaimed man's right to the pursuit of happiness and were determined to establish on earth the conditions required for man's proper existence, by the "unaided" power of their intellect.

A society based on and geared to the *conceptual* level of man's consciousness, a society dominated by a philosophy of reason, has no place for the rule of fear and guilt. Reason requires freedom, self-confidence and self-esteem. It requires the right to think and to act on the guidance of one's thinking —the right to live by one's own independent judgment. *Intellectual* freedom cannot exist without *political* freedom; political freedom cannot exist without *economic* freedom; *a free mind and a free market are corollaries.*

The unprecedented social system whose fundamentals were established by the Founding Fathers, the system which set the terms, the example and the pattern for the nineteenth century—spreading to all the countries of the civilized world —was *capitalism.*

To be exact, it was not a full, perfect, totally unregulated *laissez-faire* capitalism. Various degrees of government interference and control still remained, even in America, as deadly cracks in the system's foundations. But during the nineteenth century, the world came close to economic freedom, for the first and only time in history. The degree of any given country's economic freedom was the exact degree of its progress. America, the freest, achieved the most.

Capitalism wiped out slavery in matter and in spirit. It replaced Attila and the Witch Doctor, the looter of wealth and the purveyor of revelations, with two new types of man: the producer of wealth and the purveyor of knowledge— *the businessman and the intellectual.*

Capitalism demands the best of every man—his rationality —and rewards him accordingly. It leaves every man free to choose the work he likes, to specialize in it, to trade his product for the products of others, and to go as far on the road of achievement as his ability and ambition will carry him. His success depends on the *objective* value of his work and on the rationality of those who recognize that value. When men are free to trade, with reason and reality as their only arbiter, when no man may use physical force to extort the consent of another, it is the best product and the best judgment that win in every field of human endeavor, and raise the standard of living—and of thought—ever higher for all those who take part in mankind's productive activity.

In this complex pattern of human co-operation, two key figures act as the twin-motors of progress, the integrators of the entire system, the transmission belts that carry the achievements of the best minds to every level of society: the intellectual and the businessman.

The professional intellectual is the field agent of the army whose commander-in-chief is the *philosopher*. The intellectual carries the application of philosophical principles to every field of human endeavor. He sets a society's course by transmitting ideas from the "ivory tower" of the philosopher to the university professor—to the writer—to the artist —to the newspaperman—to the politician—to the movie maker—to the night-club singer—to the man in the street. The intellectual's specific professions are in the field of the sciences that study man, the so-called "humanities," but for that very reason his influence extends to all other professions. Those who deal with the sciences studying nature have to rely on the intellectual for philosophical guidance and information: for moral values, for social theories, for political premises, for psychological tenets and, above all, for the principles of epistemology, that crucial branch of philosophy which studies man's means of knowledge and makes all other sciences possible. The intellectual is the eyes, ears and voice of a free society: it is *his* job to observe the events of the world, to evaluate their meaning and to inform the men in all the other fields. A free society has to be an informed society. In the stagnation of feudalism, with castes and guilds of serfs repeating the same motions generation after generation, the services of traveling minstrels chanting the same old legends were sufficient. But in the racing torrent of progress which is capitalism, where the free choices of individual men determine their own lives and the course of the entire economy, where opportunities are unlimited, where discoveries are constant, where the achievements of every profession affect all the others, men need a knowledge wider than their particular specialties, they need those who can point the way to the better mousetrap—or the better cyclotron, or the better symphony, or the better view of existence. The more specialized and diversified a society, the greater its need for the integrating power of knowledge; but the acquisition of knowledge on so wide a scale is a full-time profession. A free society has to count on the honor of its intellectuals: it has to expect them to be as efficient, reliable, precise and *objective* as the printing presses and the television sets that carry their voices.

The professional businessman is the field agent of the army whose lieutenant-commander-in-chief is the *scientist.* The businessman carries scientific discoveries from the laboratory of the inventor to industrial plants, and transforms them into material products that fill men's physical needs and expand the comfort of men's existence. By creating a mass market, he makes these products available to every income level of society. By using machines, he increases the productivity of human labor, thus raising labor's economic rewards. By organizing human effort into productive enterprises, he creates employment for men of countless professions. *He* is the great liberator who, in the short span of a century and a half, has released men from bondage to their physical needs, has released them from the terrible drudgery of an eighteen-hour workday of manual labor for their barest subsistence, has released them from famines, from pestilences, from the stagnant hopelessness and terror in which most of mankind had lived in all the pre-capitalist centuries—and in which most of it still lives, in non-capitalist countries.

It is on this fundamental division of labor and of responsibility that the intellectual has defaulted. His twin brother, the businessman, has done a superlative job and has brought men to an unprecedented material prosperity. But the intellectual has sold him out, has betrayed their common source, has failed in his own job and has brought men to spiritual bankruptcy. The businessman has raised men's standard of living—but the intellectual has dropped men's standard of thought to the level of an impotent savage.

It has often been noted that mankind has achieved an enormous material progress, but has remained on the level of the primitive brute in spirit. (The solution usually offered is to abandon material progress.) The cause of the discrepancy is ignored or evaded. The cause is to be found at that crossroads of the post-Renaissance period where man's physical existence and his *philosophy* broke apart and went in different directions.

Just as a man's actions are preceded and determined by some form of idea in his mind, so a society's existential conditions are preceded and determined by the ascendancy of a certain philosophy among those whose job is to deal with ideas. The events of any given period of history are the result of the thinking of the preceding period. The nineteenth century—with its political freedom, science, industry, business, trade, all the necessary conditions of material progress—was the result and the last achievement of the intellectual power released by the Renaissance. The men engaged in those activities were still riding on the remnants of an Aristotelian influence in philosophy, particularly on an Aristotelian epistemology (more implicitly than explicitly). But they were like men living on the energy of the light rays of a distant star, who did not know (it was not their primary task to know) that that star had been extinguished.

It had been extinguished by those whose primary task was to sustain it.

From the start of the post-Renaissance period, philosophy —released from its bondage as handmaiden of theology— went seeking a new form of servitude, like a frightened slave, broken in spirit, who recoils from the responsibility of freedom. Descartes set the direction of the retreat by bringing the Witch Doctor back into philosophy. While promising a philosophical system as rational, demonstrable and scientific as mathematics, Descartes began with the basic epistemological premise of every Witch Doctor (a premise he shared explicitly with Augustine): "the prior certainty of consciousness," the belief that the *existence* of an external world is not self-evident, but must be proved by deduction from the contents of one's consciousness—which means: the concept of consciousness as some faculty other than the faculty of perception— which means: the indiscriminate contents of one's consciousness as the irreducible primary and absolute, to which reality *has* to conform. What followed was the grotesquely tragic spectacle of philosophers struggling to *prove* the existence of an external world by staring, with the Witch Doctor's blind, inward stare, at the random twists of their conceptions—then of perceptions—then of sensations.

When the medieval Witch Doctor had merely ordered men

to doubt the validity of their mind, the philosophers' rebellion against him consisted of proclaiming that they doubted whether man was conscious at all and whether anything existed for him to be conscious of.

It is at this point that Attila entered the philosophical scene.

Attila—the type of man who longs to live on the *perceptual* level of consciousness, without the "interference" of any concepts, to act on the whim and range of the moment, without the "hampering restriction" of principles or theories, without the necessity of integrating one experience with another or one moment with the next—saw his chance to escape from his subservience to the Witch Doctor, which he had always resented (to muscle in on the racket, one would have to say), and to obtain *from science* the sanction of his actions and of his psycho-epistemology. Attila, who hated and feared intellectual issues, saw his chance to take over the intellect and found his voice.

When Hume declared that he saw objects moving about, but never saw such a thing as "causality"—it was the voice of Attila that men were hearing. It was Attila's soul that spoke when Hume declared that he experienced a flow of fleeting states inside his skull, such as sensations, feelings or memories, but had never caught the experience of such a thing as *consciousness* or *self*. When Hume declared that the apparent existence of an object did not guarantee that it would not vanish spontaneously next moment, and the sunrise of today did not prove that the sun would rise tomorrow; when he declared that philosophical speculation was a game, like chess or hunting, of no significance whatever to the practical course of human existence, since reason proved that existence was unintelligible and only the ignorant maintained the illusion of knowledge—all of this accompanied by vehement opposition to the mysticism of the Witch Doctor and by protestations of loyalty to reason and science—what men were hearing was the manifesto of a philosophical movement that can be designated only as *Attila-ism*.

If it were possible for an animal to describe the content of his consciousness, the result would be a transcript of Hume's philosophy. Hume's conclusions would be the conclusions of a consciousness limited to the perceptual level of awareness, passively reacting to the experience of immediate concretes, with no capacity to form abstractions, to *integrate* perceptions into concepts, waiting in vain for the appearance of an object labeled "causality" (except that such a consciousness would not be able to draw conclusions).

To negate man's mind, it is the *conceptual* level of his consciousness that has to be invalidated. Under all the tortuous complexities, contradictions, equivocations, rationalizations of the post-Renaissance philosophy—the one consistent line, the fundamental that explains the rest, is: *a concerted attack on man's conceptual faculty*. Most philosophers did not intend to invalidate conceptual knowledge, but its defenders did more to destroy it than did its enemies. They were unable to offer a solution to the "problem of universals," that is: to define the nature and source of abstractions, to determine the relationship of concepts to perceptual data—and to prove the validity of scientific induction. Ignoring the lead of Aristotle, who had not left them a full answer to the problem, but had shown the direction and the method by which the answer could be found, the philosophers were unable to refute the Witch Doctor's claim that their concepts were as arbitrary as his whims and that their scientific knowledge had no greater metaphysical validity than his revelations.

The philosophers chose to solve the problem by conceding the Witch Doctor's claim and by surrendering to *him* the conceptual level of man's consciousness—a victory no Witch Doctor could have hoped to achieve on his own. The form of that absurd concession was the philosophers' ultimate division into two camps: those who claimed that man obtains his knowledge of the world by deducing it exclusively from concepts, which come from inside his head and are not derived from the perception of physical facts (the Rationalists) —and those who claimed that man obtains his knowledge from experience, which was held to mean: by direct perception of immediate facts, with no recourse to concepts (the Empiricists). To put it more simply: those who joined the Witch Doctor, by abandoning reality—and those who clung to reality, by abandoning their mind.

Thus reason was pushed off the philosophical scene, by default, by implication, by evasion. What had started as a serious problem between two camps of serious thinkers soon degenerated to the level where nothing was left on the field of philosophy but a battle between Witch Doctors and Attila-ists.

The man who formalized this state, and closed the door of philosophy to reason, was Immanuel Kant.

Kant gave *metaphysical* expression to the psycho-epistemology of Attila and the Witch Doctor and to their primordial existential relationship, shutting out of his universe the existence and the psycho-epistemology of the Producer. He surrendered philosophy to Attila—and insured its future delivery back into the power of the Witch Doctor. He turned the world over to Attila, but reserved to the Witch Doctor the realm of morality. Kant's expressly stated purpose was to save the morality of self-abnegation and self-sacrifice. He knew that it could not survive without a mystic base—and what it had to be saved from was *reason*.

Attila's share of Kant's universe includes this earth, physical reality, man's senses, perceptions, reason and science, all of it labeled the "phenomenal" world. The Witch Doctor's share is another, "higher," reality, labeled the "noumenal" world, and a special manifestation, labeled the "categorical imperative," which dictates to man the rules of morality and which makes itself known by means of a *feeling*, as a special sense of duty.

The "phenomenal" world, said Kant, is not real: reality, as perceived by man's mind, is a distortion. The distorting mechanism is man's conceptual faculty: man's basic concepts (such as time, space, existence) are not derived from experience or reality, but come from an automatic system of filters in his consciousness (labeled "categories" and "forms of perception") which impose their own design on his perception of the external world and make him incapable of perceiving it in any manner other than the one in which he does perceive it. This proves, said Kant, that man's concepts are only a delusion, but a *collective* delusion which no one has the power to escape. Thus reason and science are "limited," said Kant; they are valid only so long as they deal with this world, with a permanent, pre-determined collective delusion (and thus the criterion of reason's validity was switched from the *objective* to the *collective*), but they are impotent to deal with the fundamental, metaphysical issues of existence, which belong to the "noumenal" world. The "noumenal" world is unknowable; it is the world of "real" reality, "superior" truth and "things in themselves" or "things as they are"—which means: things as they are *not* perceived by man.

Even apart from the fact that Kant's theory of the "categories" as the source of man's concepts was a preposterous invention, his argument amounted to a negation, not only of man's consciousness, but of *any* consciousness, of consciousness as such. His argument, in essence, ran as follows: man is *limited* to a consciousness of a specific nature, which perceives by specific means and no others, therefore, his consciousness is not valid; man is blind, because he has eyes—deaf, because he has ears—deluded, because he has a mind —and the things he perceives do not exist, *because* he perceives them.

As to Kant's version of morality, it was appropriate to the kind of zombies that would inhabit that kind of universe: it consisted of total, abject *selflessness*. An action is moral, said Kant, only if one has no desire to perform it, but performs it out of a sense of *duty* and derives no benefit from it of any sort, neither material nor spiritual; a benefit destroys the moral value of an action. (Thus, if one has no desire to be evil, one cannot be good; if one has, one can.)

Those who accept any part of Kant's philosophy—metaphysical, epistemological or moral—deserve it.

If one finds the present state of the world unintelligible and inexplicable, one can begin to understand it by realizing that the dominant intellectual influence today is still Kant's —and that all the leading modern schools of philosophy are derived from a Kantian base.

The popular slang expression "head-shrinker," applied to psychologists, is much more literally applicable to Kant: observe the sharp drop in the intellectual stature of the post-Kantian philosophers, and the progressively thickening veil of grayness, superficiality, casuistry that descends on the history of philosophy thereafter—like a fog enveloping a sluggish river that runs thinner and thinner and finally vanishes in the swamps of the twentieth century.

The major line of philosophers rejected Kant's "noumenal" world quiet speedily, but they accepted his "phenomenal" world and carried it to its logical consequences: the view of reality as mere appearance; the view of man's conceptual faculty as a mechanism for producing arbitrary "constructs" not derived from experience or facts; the view of rational certainty as impossible, of science as unprovable, of man's mind as impotent—and, above all, the equation of morality with selflessness. They rejected the root or cause of Kant's system, but accepted all of its deadly effects. They accepted it as some monstrous spider hanging in midair, in a web of unintelligible, almost unreadable verbiage—and, today, few people know that that spider is not supported by a single thread of proof.

Such was the intellectual equipment with which philosophers approached the task of observing the unprecedented historical events of the nineteenth century, and the responsibility of providing guidance for the new, free society of capitalism.

While scientists were performing astounding feats of disciplined reason, breaking down the barriers of the "unknowable" in every field of knowledge, charting the course of light rays in space or the course of blood in the capillaries of man's body—what philosophy was offering them, as interpretation of and guidance for their achievements was the plain Witch-doctory of Hegel, who proclaimed that matter does not exist at all, that everything is Idea (not somebody's idea, just *Idea*), and that this Idea operates by the dialectical process of a new "super-logic" which proves that *contradictions* are the law of reality, that A is non-A, and that omniscience about the physical universe (including electricity, gravitation, the solar system, etc.) is to be derived, not from the observation of facts, but from the contemplation of that Idea's triple somersaults inside his, Hegel's, mind. *This* was offered as a philosophy of reason.

While businessmen were rising to spectacular achievements of creative ability and self-confidently ambitious courage, challenging the primordial dogma of man's poverty and misery on earth, breaking open the trade routes of the world, releasing mankind's productive energy and placing in its service the liberating power of machines (against the scornful resistance of loafing, ex-feudal aristocrats and the destructive violence of those who were to profit most: the workers)—what philosophy was offering, as an evaluation of their achievements and as guidance for the rest of society was the pure Attila-ism of Marx, who proclaimed that the mind does not exist, that everything is matter, that matter develops itself by the dialectical process of its own "super-logic" of contradictions, and what is true today, will not be true tomorrow, that the material tools of production determine men's "ideological superstructure" (which means: machines create men's thinking, not the other way around), that muscular labor is the source of wealth, that physical force is the only practical means of existence, and that the seizure of the omnipotent machines will transfer omnipotence to the rule of brute violence. Never had Attila's psycho-epistemology been transcribed so accurately. *This* was offered as a philosophy of history and of political economy.

What was offered as philosophical antidote to those who would not accept these theories?

As a defense against the Witch-doctory of Kant and Hegel, the *businessman* was offered the neo-mystic Attila-ism of the Pragmatists. They declared that philosophy must be *practical* and that practicality consists of dispensing with all absolute principles and standards—that there is no such thing as objective reality or permanent truth—that *truth is that which works,* and its validity can be judged only by its consequences—that no facts can be known with certainty in advance, and anything may be tried by rule-of-thumb—that reality is not firm, but fluid and "indeterminate," that there is no such thing as a distinction between an external world and a consciousness (between the perceived and the perceiver), there is only an undifferentiated package-deal labeled "experience," and whatever one wishes to be true, *is* true, whatever one wishes to exist, *does* exist, provided it works or makes one feel better.

A later school of more Kantian Pragmatists amended this philosophy as follows. If there is no such thing as an objective reality, men's metaphysical choice is whether the selfish, dictatorial whims of an individual or the democratic whims of a collective are to shape that plastic goo which the ignorant call "reality," therefore this school decided that *objectivity consists of collective subjectivism*—that knowledge is to be gained by means of public polls among special elites of "competent investigators" who can "predict and control" reality—that whatever people wish to be true, *is* true, whatever people wish to exist, *does* exist, and anyone who holds any firm convictions of his own is an arbitrary, mystic dogmatist, since reality is indeterminate and people determine its actual nature.

The *scientist* was offered a slightly different version of philosophy. As a defense against the Witch-doctory of Hegel, who claimed universal omniscience, the scientist was offered the combined neo-mystic Witch-doctory and Attila-ism of the Logical Positivists. They assured him that such concepts as metaphysics or existence or reality or thing or matter or mind are meaningless—let the mystics care whether they exist or not, a scientist does not have to know it; the task of theoretical science is the manipulation of symbols, and scientists are the special elite whose symbols have the magic power of making reality conform to their will ("matter is that which fits mathematical equations"). Knowledge, they said, consists, not of facts, but of *words*, words unrelated to objects, words of an arbitrary social convention, as an irreducible primary; thus knowledge is merely a matter of manipulating language. The job of scientists, they said, is not the study of reality, but the creation of arbitrary constructs by means of arbitrary sounds, and any construct is as valid as another, since the criterion of validity is only "convenience" and the definition of science is "that which the scientists do." But this omnipotent power, surpassing the dreams of ancient numerologists or of medieval alchemists, was granted to the scientist by philosophical Attila-ism on two conditions: *a.* that he never claim certainty for his knowledge, since certainty is unknowable to man, and that he claim, instead, "percentages of probability," not troubling himself with such questions as how one calculates percentages of the unknowable; *b.* that he claim as absolute knowledge the proposition that all values lie outside the sphere of science, that reason is impotent to deal with morality, that moral values are a matter of subjective choice, dictated by one's feelings, not one's mind.

The great treason of the philosophers was that they never stepped out of the Middle Ages: they never challenged the Witch Doctor's code of morality. They were willing to doubt the existence of physical objects, they were willing to doubt the validity of their own senses, they were willing to defy the authority of absolute monarchies, they were willing (occasionally) to proclaim themselves to be skeptics or agnostics or atheists—but they were not willing to doubt the doctrine that man is a sacrificial animal, that he has no right to exist for his own sake, that service to others is the only justification of his existence and that *self-sacrifice* is his highest moral duty, virtue and value.

Under all its countless guises, variations and adaptations, that doctrine—best designated as the morality of altruism—has come from prehistóric swamps to New York City, unchanged. In savage societies, men practiced the ritual of human sacrifices, immolating individual men on sacrificial altars, for the sake of what they regarded as their collective, tribal good. Today, they are still doing it, only the agony is slower and the slaughter greater—but the doctrine that demands it and sanctions it, is the same doctrine of moral cannibalism.

The philosophers preserved it, by leaving the subject of morality to the mystics—or by consigning it to the province of subjective *feelings*, which means: to the mystics—or by the vehement rejection of reason's capacity to deal with moral values and the branding of all value-judgments as "unscientific," which means: the reaffirmation and perpetuation of the mystics' monopoly on morality—or, worst of all, by accepting the mystics' moral code in its irrational entirety, then translating it into earthly terms and propagating it in the name of reason.

The convolutions of this last attempt provide what is, perhaps, the most grotesquely terrible chapter in the history of Western thought. The political "me-too-ism," abjectly displayed by the "conservatives" of today toward their brazenly socialistic adversaries, is only the result and the feeble reflection of the ethical "me-too-ism" displayed by the philosophers of the nineteenth and twentieth centuries, by the alleged champions of reason, toward the Witch Doctors of morality.

Auguste Comte, the founder of Positivism, the champion of science, advocated a "rational," "scientific" social system based on the total subjugation of the individual to the collective, including a "Religion of Humanity" which substituted *Society* for the Gods or gods who collect the blood of sacrificial victims. It is not astonishing that Comte was the coiner of the term *Altruism*, which means: the placing of others above self, of their interests above one's own.

Nietzsche's rebellion against altruism consisted of replacing the sacrifice of oneself to others by the sacrifice of others to oneself. He proclaimed that the ideal man is moved, not by reason, but by his "blood," by his innate instincts, feelings and will to power—that he is predestined by birth to rule others and sacrifice them to himself, while *they* are predestined by birth to be his victims and slaves—that reason, logic, principles are futile and debilitating, that morality is useless, that the "superman" is "beyond good and evil," that he is a "beast of prey" whose ultimate standard is nothing but his own whim. Thus Nietzsche's rejection of the Witch Doctor consisted of elevating Attila into a moral ideal—which meant: a double surrender of morality to the Witch Doctor.

Jeremy Bentham, the champion of capitalism, defended it

by proclaiming "the greatest happiness of the greatest number" as its moral justification—and propounded a "hedonistic calculus" for men's moral guidance, which enunciated the principle that before taking any action one must consider all the possible forms and amounts of happiness and unhappiness to accrue to all the people possibly to be affected by the consequences of one's action (including oneself as one unit among the dozens or hundreds or millions), one must compute them all, then act accordingly and sacrifice the "hedonistic" minority to the majority.

Herbert Spencer, another champion of capitalism, chose to decide that the theory of evolution and of adaptation to environment was the key to man's morality—and declared that the moral justification of capitalism was the survival of the species, of the human *race;* that whoever was of no value to the race, had to perish; that man's morality consisted of adapting oneself to one's *social* environment, and seeking one's own happiness in the welfare of society; and that the automatic processes of evolution would eventually obliterate the distinction between selfishness and unselfishness.

And when Karl Marx, the most consistent translator of the altruist morality into practical action and political theory, advocated a society where all would be sacrificed to all, starting with the immediate immolation of the able, the intelligent, the successful and the wealthy—whatever opposition he did encounter, nobody opposed him on *moral* grounds. Predominantly, he was granted the status of a noble, but impractical, *idealist.*

The great treason of the philosophers was that they, the thinkers, defaulted on the responsibility of providing a rational society with a code of *rational morality.* They, whose job it was to discover and define man's moral values, stared at the brilliant torrent of man's released energy and had nothing better to offer for its guidance than the Witch Doctor's morality of human sacrifices—of self-denial, self-abasement, self-immolation—of suffering, guilt and death.

The failure of philosophers to challenge the Witch Doctor's morality, has cost them their kingdom: philosophy. The relationship of reason and morality is reciprocal: the man who accepts the role of a sacrificial animal, will not achieve the self-confidence necessary to uphold the validity of his mind—the man who doubts the validity of his mind, will not achieve the self-esteem necessary to uphold the value of his person and to discover the moral premises that make man's value possible.

The intellectuals share the philosophers' guilt. The intellectuals—all those whose professions deal with the "humanities" and require a firm philosophical base—have known for a long time that no such base existed. They knew that they were functioning in a philosophical vacuum and that the currency they were passing was rubber checks which would bounce, some day, wrecking their culture.

One can never know, only surmise, what tragedies, despair and silent devastation have been going on for over a century in the invisible underground of the intellectual professions—in the souls of their practitioners—nor what incalculable potential of human ability and integrity perished in those hidden, lonely conflicts. The young minds who came to the field of the intellect with the inarticulate sense of a crusade, seeking rational answers to the problems of achieving a meaningful human existence, found a philosophical con game in place of guidance and leadership. Some of them gave up the field of ideas, in hopeless, indignant frustration, and vanished into the silence of subjectivity. Others gave in, and saw their eagerness turn into bitterness, their quest into apathy, their crusade into a cynical racket. They condemned themselves to the chronic anxiety of a con man dreading exposure when they accepted the roles of enlightened leaders, while knowing that their knowledge rested on nothing but fog and that its only validation was somebody's feelings.

They, the standard bearers of the mind, found themselves dreading reason as an enemy, logic as a pursuer, thought as an avenger. They, the proponents of ideas, found themselves clinging to the belief that ideas were impotent: their choice was the futility of a charlatan or the guilt of a traitor. They were not mediocrities when they began their careers; they were pretentious mediocrities when they ended. The exceptions are growing rarer with every generation. No one can accept with psychological impunity the function of a Witch Doctor under the banner of the intellect.

With nothing but quicksands to stand on—the shifting mixture of Witch-doctory and Attila-ism as their philosophical base—the intellectuals were unable to grasp, to identify or to evaluate the historical drama taking place before them: the industrial revolution and capitalism. They were like men who did not see the splendor of a rocket bursting over their heads, because their eyes were lowered in guilt. It was *their* job to see and to explain—to a society of men stumbling dazedly out of a primeval dungeon—the cause and the meaning of the events that were sweeping them faster and farther than the motion of all the centuries behind hem. The intellectuals did not choose to see.

The men in the other professions were not able to step back and observe. If some men found themselves leaving their farms for a chance to work in a factory, that was all they knew. If their children now had a chance to survive beyond the age of ten (child mortality had been about fifty percent in the pre-capitalist era), they were not able to identify the cause. They could not tell why the periodic famines—that had been striking every twenty years to wipe out the "surplus" population which pre-capitalist economies could not feed—now came to an end, as did the carnages of religious wars, nor why fear seemed to be lifting away from people's voices and from the streets of growing cities, nor why an enormous exultation was suddenly sweeping the world. The intellectuals did not choose to tell them.

The intellectuals, or their predominant majority, remained centuries behind their time: still seeking the favor of noble protectors, some of them were bewailing the "vulgarity" of commercial pursuits, scoffing at those whose wealth was "new," and, simultaneously, blaming these new wealth-makers for all the poverty inherited from the centuries ruled by the owners of nobly "non-commercial" wealth. Others were denouncing machines as "inhuman," and factories as a blemish on the beauty of the countryside (where gallows had formerly stood at the crossroads). Still others were calling for a movement "back to nature," to the handicrafts, to the Middle Ages. And some were attacking scientists for inquiring into forbidden "mysteries" and interfering with God's design.

The victim of the intellectuals' most infamous injustice was the businessman.

Having accepted the premises, the moral values and the position of Witch Doctors, the intellectuals were unwilling to differentiate between the businessman and Attila, between the producer of wealth and the looter. Like the Witch Doctor, they scorned and dreaded the realm of material reality, feeling secretly inadequate to deal with it. Like the Witch Doctor's, their secret vision (almost their feared and envied ideal) of a practical, successful man, a true master of reality, was Attila; like the Witch Doctor, they believed that force, fraud, lies, plunder, expropriation, enslavement, murder were *practical*. So they did not inquire into the source of wealth or ever ask what made it possible (they had been taught that causality is an illusion and that only the immediate moment is real). They took it as their axiom, as an irreducible primary, that wealth can be acquired only by force—and that a fortune *as such* is the proof of plunder, with no further distinctions or inquiries necessary.

With their eyes still fixed on the Middle Ages, they were maintaining this in the midst of a period when a greater amount of wealth than had ever before existed in the world was being brought into existence all around them. If the men who produced that wealth were thieves, from whom had they stolen it? Under all the shameful twists of their evasions, the intellectuals' answer was: from those who had *not* produced it. They were refusing to acknowledge the industrial revolution (they are still refusing today). They were refusing to admit into their universe what neither Attila nor the Witch Doctor can afford to admit: the existence of man, the Producer.

Evading the difference between production and looting, they called the businessman a robber. Evading the difference between freedom and compulsion, they called him a slave driver. Evading the difference between reward and terror, they called him an exploiter. Evading the difference between pay checks and guns, they called him an autocrat. Evading the difference between trade and force, they called him a tyrant. The most crucial issue they had to evade was the difference between the *earned* and the *unearned*.

Ignoring the existence of the faculty they were betraying, the faculty of discrimination, the intellect, they refused to identify the fact that industrial wealth was the product of man's mind: that an incalculable amount of intellectual power, of creative intelligence, of disciplined energy, of human genius had gone into the creation of industrial fortunes. They could not afford to identify it, because they could not afford to admit the fact that the intellect is a *practical* faculty, a guide to man's successful existence on earth, and that its task is the study of reality (as well as the production of wealth), not the contemplation of unintelligible feelings nor a special monopoly on the "unknowable."

The Witch Doctor's morality of altruism—the morality that damns all those who achieve success or enjoyment on earth—provided the intellectuals with the means to make a virtue of evasion. It gave them a weapon that disarmed their victims; it gave them an automatic substitute for self-esteem, and a chance at an *unearned* moral stature. They proclaimed themselves to be the defenders of the poor against the rich, righteously evading the fact that the rich were not Attilas any longer—and the defenders of the weak against the strong, righteously evading the fact that the strength involved was not the strength of brute muscles any longer, but the strength of man's mind.

But while the intellectuals regarded the businessman as Attila, the businessman would not behave as they, from the position of Witch Doctors, expected Attila to behave: he was impervious to their power. The businessman was as bewildered by events as the rest of mankind, he had no time to grasp his own historical role, he had no moral weapons, no voice, no defense, and—knowing no morality but the altruist code, yet knowing also that he was functioning against it, that self-sacrifice was *not* his role—he was helplessly vulnerable to the intellectuals' attack. He would have welcomed eagerly the guidance of Aristotle, but had no use for Immanuel Kant. That which today is called "common sense" is the remnant of an Aristotelian influence, and *that* was the businessman's only form of philosophy. The businessman asked for proof and expected things to make sense—an expectation that kicked the intellectuals into the category of the unemployed. They had nothing to offer to a man who did not buy any shares of any version of the "noumenal" world.

To understand the course the intellectuals chose to take, it is important to remember the Witch Doctor's psycho-epistemology and his relationship to Attila: the Witch Doctor expects Attila to be his protector against reality, against the necessity of rational cognition, and, at the same time, he expects to rule his own protector, who needs an *unintelligible* mystic sanction as a narcotic to relieve his chronic guilt. They derive their mutual security, not from any form of strength, but from the fact that each has a hold on the other's secret weakness. It is not the security of two traders, who count on the *values* they offer each other, but the security of two blackmailers, who count on each other's *fear*.

The Witch Doctor feels like a metaphysical outcast in a

capitalist society—as if he were pushed into some limbo outside of any universe he cares to recognize. He has no means to deal with innocence; he can get no hold on a man who does not seek to live in guilt, on a businessman who is confident of his ability to earn his living—who takes pride in his work and in the value of his product—who drives himself with inexhaustible energy and limitless ambition to do better and still better and ever better—who is willing to bear penalties for his mistakes and expects rewards for his achievements—who looks at the universe with the fearless eagerness of a child, knowing it to be intelligible—who demands straight lines, clear terms, precise definitions—who stands in full sunlight and has no use for the murky fog of the hidden, the secret, the unnamed, the furtively evocative, for any code of signals from the psycho-epistemology of guilt.

What the businessman offered to the intellectuals was the spiritual counterpart of his own activity, that which the Witch Doctor dreads most: the freedom of the market place of ideas.

To live by the work of one's mind, to offer men the products of one's thinking, to provide them with new knowledge, to stand on nothing but the merit of one's ideas and to rely on nothing but *objective* truth, in a market open to any man who is willing to think and has to judge, accept or reject on his own—is a task that only a man on the conceptual level of psycho-epistemology can welcome or fulfill. It is not the place for a Witch Doctor nor for any mystic "elite." A Witch Doctor has to live by the favor of a protector, by a special dispensation, by a reserved monopoly, by exclusion, by suppression, by *censorship.*

Having accepted the philosophy and the psycho-epistemology of the Witch Doctor, the intellectuals had to cut the ground from under their own feet and turn against their own historical distinction: against the first chance men had ever had to make a professional living by means of the intellect. When the intellectuals rebelled against the "commercialism" of a capitalist society, what they were specifically rebelling against was the open market of ideas, where *feelings* were not accepted and ideas were expected to demonstrate their validity, where the risks were great, injustices were possible and no protector existed but objective reality.

Just as Attila, since the Renaissance, was looking for a Witch Doctor of his own, so the intellectuals, since the industrial revolution, were looking for an Attila of their own. The altruist morality brought them together and gave them the weapon they needed. The field where they found each other was Socialism.

It was not the businessmen or the industrialists or the workers or the labor unions or the remnants of the feudal aristocracy that began the revolt against freedom and the demand for the return of the absolute state: it was the intellectuals. It was the alleged guardians of reason who brought mankind back to the rule of brute force.

Growing throughout the nineteenth century, originated in and directed from intellectual salons, sidewalk cafés, basement beer joints and university classrooms, the industrial counter-revolution united the Witch Doctors and the Attilaists. They demanded the right to enforce *ideas* at the point of a gun, that is: through the power of government, and compel the submission of others to the views and wishes of those who would gain control of the government's machinery. They extolled the State as the "Form of the Good," with man as its abject servant, and they proposed as many variants of the socialist state as there had been of the altruist morality. But, in both cases, the variations merely played with the surface, while the cannibal essence remained the same: socialism is the doctrine that man has no right to exist for his own sake, that his life and his work do not belong to *him*, but belong to society, that the only justification of his existence is his service to society, and that society may dispose of him in any way it pleases for the sake of whatever it deems to be its own tribal, collective good.

It is only the Attila-ist, pragmatist, positivist, anti-conceptual mentality—which grants no validity to abstractions, no meaning to principles and no power to ideas—that can still wonder why a theoretical doctrine of that kind had to lead in practice to the torrent of blood and brute, non-human horror of such socialist societies as Nazi Germany and Soviet Russia. Only the Attila-ist mentality can still claim that nobody can prove that these had to be the *necessary* results— or still try to blame it on the "imperfection" of human nature or on the evil of some specific gang who "betrayed a noble ideal," and still promise that its own gang would do it better and make it work—or still mumble in a quavering voice that the motive was love of humanity.

The pretenses have worn thin, the evasions do not work

any longer; the intellectuals are aware of their guilt, but are still struggling to evade its cause and to pass it on to the universe at large, to man's metaphysically predestined impotence.

Guilt and fear are the disintegrators of a man's consciousness or of a society's culture. Today, America's culture is being splintered into disintegration by the three injunctions which permeate our intellectual atmosphere and which are typical of guilt: don't look—don't judge—don't be certain.

The psycho-epistemological meaning and implementation of these three are: don't integrate—don't evaluate—give up.

The last stand of Attila-ism, both in philosophy and in science, is the concerted assertion of all the neo-mystics that integration is impossible and unscientific. The escape from the conceptual level of consciousness, the progressive contraction of man's vision down to Attila's range, has now reached its ultimate climax. Withdrawing from reality and responsibility, the neo-mystics proclaim that no entities exist, only relationships, and that one may study relationships without anything to relate, and, simultaneously, that every datum is single and discrete, and no datum can ever be related to any other data—that context is irrelevant, that anything may be proved or disproved in midair and midstream, and the narrower the subject of study, the better—that myopia is the hallmark of a thinker or a scientist.

System-building—the integration of knowledge into a coherent sum and a consistent view of reality—is denounced by all the Attila-ists as irrational, mystical and unscientific. This is Attila's perennial way of surrendering to the Witch Doctor—and it explains why so many scientists are turning to God or to such flights of mysticism of their own as would make even an old-fashioned Witch Doctor blush. No consciousness can accept disintegration as a normal and permanent state. Science was born as a result and consequence of philosophy; it cannot survive without a philosophical (particularly epistemological) base. If philosophy perishes, science will be next to go.

The abdication of philosophy is all but complete. Today's philosophers, *qua* Witch Doctors, declare that nobody can define what *is* philosophy or what is its specific task, but this need not prevent anyone from practicing it as a profession. *Qua* Attila-ists, they declare that the use of wide abstractions or concepts is the prerogative of the layman or of the ignorant or of the man in the street—while a philosopher is one who, knowing all the difficulties involved in the problem of abstractions, deals with nothing but concretes.

The injunction "don't judge" is the ultimate climax of the altruist morality which, today, can be seen in its naked essence. When men plead for forgiveness, for the nameless, cosmic forgiveness of an unconfessed evil, when they react with instantaneous compassion to any guilt, to the perpetrators of any atrocity, while turning away indifferently from the bleeding bodies of the victims and the innocent—one may see the actual purpose, motive and psychological appeal of the altruist code. When these same compassionate men turn with snarling hatred upon anyone who pronounces moral judgments, when they scream that the only evil is the determination to fight against evil—one may see the kind of moral blank check that the altruist morality hands out.

Perhaps the most craven attitude of all is the one expressed by the injunction "don't be certain." As stated explicitly by many intellectuals, it is the suggestion that if nobody is certain of anything, if nobody holds any firm convictions, if everybody is willing to give in to everybody else, no dictator will rise among us and we will escape the destruction sweeping the rest of the world. This is the secret voice of the Witch Doctor confessing that he sees a dictator, an Attila, as a man of confident strength and uncompromising conviction. Nothing but a psycho-epistemological panic can blind such intellectuals to the fact that a dictator, like any thug, runs from the first sign of confident resistance; that he can rise *only* in a society of precisely such uncertain, compliant, shaking compromisers as they advocate, a society that invites a thug to take over; and that the task of resisting an Attila can be accomplished only by men of intransigent conviction and moral certainty—not by chickens hiding their heads in the sand ("ostrich" is too big and dignified a metaphor for this instance).

And, paving the way for Attila, the intellectuals are still repeating, not by conviction any longer, but by rote, that the growth of government power is not an abridgment of freedom—that the demand of one group for an unearned share of another group's income is not socialism—that the destruction of property rights will not affect any other rights —that man's mind, intelligence, creative ability are a *"national resource"* (like mines, forests, waterfalls, buffalo reserves and national parks) to be taken over, subsidized and disposed of by the government—that businessmen are selfish autocrats because they are struggling to preserve freedom, while the "liberals" are the true champions of liberty because they are fighting for more government controls—that the fact that we are sliding down a road which has destroyed every other country, does not prove that it will destroy ours—that dictatorship is not dictatorship if nobody calls it by that *abstract* name—and that none of us can help it, anyway.

Nobody believes any of it any longer, yet nobody opposes it. To oppose anything, one needs a firm set of principles, which means: a philosophy.

If America perishes, it will perish by intellectual default. There is no diabolical conspiracy to destroy it: no conspiracy could be big enough and strong enough. Such cafeteria-socialist conspiracies as do undoubtedly exist are groups of scared, neurotic mediocrities who find themselves pushed into national leadership because nobody else steps forward; they are like pickpockets who merely intended to snatch a welfare-regulation or two and who suddenly find that their victim is unconscious, that they are alone in an enormous mansion of fabulous wealth, with all the doors open and a seasoned burglar's job on their hands; watch them now screaming that they didn't mean it, that they had never advocated the nationalization of a country's economy. As to the communist conspirators in the service of Soviet Russia, they are the best illustration of victory by default: their successes are handed to them by the concessions of their victims. There is no national movement for socialism or dictatorship in America, no "man on horseback" or popular demagogue, nothing but fumbling compromisers and frightened opportunists. Yet we are moving toward full, totalitarian socialism, with worn, cynical voices telling us that such is the irresistible trend of history. History, fate and malevolent conspiracy are easier to believe than the actual truth: that we are moved by nothing but the sluggish inertia of unfocused minds.

Collectivism, as a social ideal, is dead, but capitalism has not yet been discovered. It cannot be discovered by the psycho-epistemology of Witch Doctors and Attila-ists—and as to the businessman, he is struggling to forget that he had ever known it. That is *his* guilt.

The businessman, historically, had started as the victim of the intellectuals; but no injustice or exploitation can succeed for long without the sanction of the victim. The businessman, who could not accept the intellectual leadership of post-Kantian Witch Doctors, made his fatal error when he conceded to them the field of the intellect. He gave them the benefit of the doubt, at his own expense: he concluded that their meaningless verbiage could not be as bad as it sounded to *him*, that he lacked understanding, but had no stomach for trying to understand that sort of stuff and would leave it respectfully alone. No Witch Doctor could have hoped for a deadlier concession.

By becoming anti-intellectual, the businessman condemned himself to the position of an Attila. By restricting his goals, concerns and vision exclusively to his specific productive activity, he was forced to restrict his interests to Attila's narrow range of the physical, the material, the immediately present. Thus he tore himself in two by an inner contradiction: he functioned on a confidently rational, conceptual level of psycho-epistemology in business, but repressed all the other aspects of his life and thought, letting himself he carried passively along by the general cultural current, in the semi-unfocused, perceptual-level daze of a man who considers himself impotent to judge what he perceives. It is thus that he turned too often into the tragic phenomenon of a genius in business who is a Babbitt in his private life.

He repressed and renounced any interest in ideas, any quest for intellectual values or moral principles. He could not accept the altruist morality, as no man of self-esteem can accept it, and he found no other moral philosophy. He lived by a subjective code of his own—the code of justice, the code of a fair trader—without knowing what a superlative moral virtue it represented. His private version or understanding of altruism—particularly in America—took the form of an enormous generosity, the joyous, innocent, benevolent generosity of a self-confident man, who is too innocent to suspect that he is hated for his success, that the moralists of altruism want him to pay financial tributes, not as kindness, but as atonement for the guilt of having succeeded. There were exceptions; there were businessmen who did accept the full philosophical meaning of altruism and its ugly burden of guilt, but they were not the majority.

They are the majority today. No man or group of men can live indefinitely under the pressure of moral injustice: they have to rebel or give in. Most of the businessmen gave in; it would have taken a philosopher to provide them with the intellectual weapons of rebellion, but they had given up any interest in philosophy. They accepted the burden of an unearned guilt; they accepted the brand of "vulgar materialists"; they accepted the accusations of "predatory greed"— predatory toward the wealth which *they* had created, greed for the fortunes which, but for them, would not have existed. As a result, consciously or subconsciously, they were driven to the cynical bitterness of the conviction that men are irrational, that reason is impotent in human relationships, that the field of ideas is some dark, gigantic, incomprehensible fraud.

No one can accept unearned guilt with psychological impunity. Starting as the most courageous class of men in history, the businessmen have slipped slowly into the position of men motivated by chronic fear—in all the social, political, moral, *intellectual* aspects of their existence. Their public policy consists of appeasing their worst enemies, placating their most contemptible attackers, trying to make terms with their own destroyers, pouring money into the support of leftist publications and "liberal" politicians, placing avowed collectivists in charge of their public relations and then voicing—in banquet speeches and full-page ads—socialistic protestations that selfless service to society is their only goal, and altruistic apologies for the fact that they still keep two or three percent of profit out of their multi-million-dollar enterprises.

There are many different motives behind that policy. Some men are moved by actual guilt: they are the new type of businessmen, the product of a "mixed" economy, who make fortunes, not by productive ability and competition in a free market, but by political pull, by government favors, subsidies, franchises and special privileges; these are psycho-epistemologically and economically closer to Attila than to the Producer, and have good reason to feel guilty. Others are forced reluctantly into a mixed position, where they still live by productive ability, yet have to depend on government favors in order to function; these are the closest to the position of self-destroyers. The majority of businessmen—perhaps the ablest and best—work in silence and are never heard from publicly. Most businessmen have probably given up the expectation of any justice from the public. But there is one motive which is shared by too many businessmen and which is the penalty for renouncing the intellect: an unconfessed fear of ideas under the professed conviction that ideas are futile, which leads to a nervously stubborn evasiveness, an anxious feeling or hope that wealth as such is power, that only material possessions are of practical importance.

Today, the businessman and the intellectual face each other with the mutual fear and the mutual contempt of Attila and the Witch Doctor. The businessman has lost confidence in all theories, and functions on a range-of-the-moment expediency, not daring to look at the future. The intellectual has cut himself off from reality and plays a futile word-game with ideas, not daring to look at the past. The businessman considers the intellectual impractical; the intellectual considers the businessman immoral. But, secretly, each of them believes that the other possesses a mysterious faculty *he* lacks, that the other is the true master of reality, the true exponent of the power to deal with existence.

It is by this mutual attitude and the philosophical premises from which it comes that they are destroying each other. The major share of the guilt belongs to the intellectual: philosophical leadership was *his* responsibility, which he betrayed and is now deserting under fire.

The most grotesquely anachronistic and atavistic spectacle in history is the spectacle of the modern intellectuals raising the primordial voice of the Witch Doctor and, in the midst of an industrial civilization, wailing about the hopeless misery of life on earth, the depravity of man, the impotence of man's mind, the ignoble vulgarity of material pursuits, and the nobility of longing for the supernatural.

The echoes answering them are the voices of the plain, medieval Witch Doctors that are beginning to be heard again, preaching the doctrine of man's innate, preordained impotence, of humility, passivity, submission and resignation— here, in New York City, the greatest monument to the potency of man's mind—and proclaiming that all the disasters of the modern age are man's punishment for the pride of relying on his intellect, for his attempt to improve his condition, to establish a rational society and to achieve a perfect way of life on earth.

On a recent television panel discussion, an alleged conservative intellectual was asked to define the difference between a "conservative" and a "liberal." He answered that a "liberal" is one who does not believe in Original Sin. To which a liberal intellectual replied hastily: "Oh, yes, we do!" —but proceeded to add that the liberals believe they can improve men's life *just a little*.

Such is the bankruptcy of a culture.

It is into the midst of this dismal gray vacuum that the New Intellectuals must step—and must challenge the worshippers of doom, resignation and death, with an attitude best expressed by a paraphrase of an ancient salute: "We who are *not* about to die . . ."

Who are to be the New Intellectuals? Any man or woman who is willing to think. All those who know that man's life must be guided by reason, those who value their own life and are not willing to surrender it to the cult of despair in the modern jungle of cynical impotence, just as they are not willing to surrender the world to the Dark Ages and the rule of the brutes.

The need for intellectual leadership was never as great as now. No human being who has a trace of personal worth can be willing to surrender his life without lifting a hand—or a mind—to defend it, particularly not in America, the country based on the premise of man's self-reliance and self-esteem. Americans have known how to erect a superlative material achievement in the midst of an untouched wilderness, against the resistance of savage tribes. What we need today is to erect a corresponding *philosophical* structure, without which the material greatness cannot survive. A skyscraper cannot stand on crackerbarrels, nor on wall mottoes, nor on full-page ads, nor on prayers, nor on meta-language. The new wilderness to reclaim is philosophy, now all but deserted, with the weeds of prehistoric doctrines rising again to swallow the ruins. To support a culture, nothing less than a new philosophical foundation will do. The present state of the world is not the proof of philosophy's impotence, but the proof of philosophy's power. It is philosophy that has brought men to this state—it is only philosophy that can lead them out.

Those who could become the New Intellectuals are America's hidden assets; their number is probably greater than anyone can estimate; they exist in every profession, even among the present intellectuals. But they are scattered in silent helplessness throughout the country, or hidden in that underground which, in human history, has too often swallowed the best of men's potential: subjectivity. They are the men who have long since lost respect for the cultural standards to which they conform, but who hide their own convictions or repress their ideas or suppress their minds, each feeling that he has no chance against the others, each serving as both victim and destroyer. The New Intellectuals will be those men who will come out into the open and have the courage to break that vicious circle.

If they glance at the state of our culture, they will see that the entire miserable show is kept up by nothing but routine and pretense, which disguise bewilderment and fear: nobody dares to take the first new step, everybody waits for his neighbor's initiative. If a society reaches the stage where every man accepts the feeling that he is "a stranger and afraid in a world [he] never made," the world it gives up will be made by Attila. The greatest need today is for men who are not strangers to reality, because they are not afraid of thought. The New Intellectuals will be those who will take the initiative and the responsibility: they will check their own philosophical premises, identify their convictions, integrate their ideas into coherence and consistency, then offer to the country a view of existence to which the wise and honest can repair.

The New Intellectual will be the man who lives up to the exact meaning of his title: a man who is guided by his *intellect*—not a zombie guided by feelings, instincts, urges, wishes, whims or revelations. Ending the rule of Attila and the Witch Doctor, he will discard the basic premise that made them possible: the soul-body dichotomy. He will discard its irrational conflicts and contradictions, such as: mind *versus* heart, thought *versus* action, reality *versus* desire, the practical *versus* the moral. He will be an *integrated man*, that is: a thinker who is a man of action. He will know that ideas divorced from consequent action are fraudulent, and that action divorced from ideas is suicidal. He will know that the conceptual level of psycho-epistemology—the volitional level of reason and thought—is the basic necessity of man's survival and his greatest moral virtue. He will know that men need philosophy for the purpose of *living on earth*.

The New Intellectual will be a reunion of the twins who should never have been separated: the intellectual and the businessman. He can come from among the best—that is: the most rational—men who may still exist in both camps. In place of an involuntary Witch Doctor and a reluctant

Attila, the reunion will produce two new types: the practical thinker and the philosophical businessman.

The best among the present intellectuals should consider the tremendous power which they are holding, but have never fully exercised or understood. If any man among them feels that he is the helpless, ineffectual stepson of a "materialistic" culture that grants him neither wealth nor recognition, let him remember the meaning of his title: his power is his *intellect* not his feelings, emotions or intuitions. It is not the businessmen who have robbed him of efficacy, but those of his colleagues who have degraded his profession to the level of soothsayers, tea-leaf readers and jungle oracles. Let him break with the neo-mystics; let him realize that ideas are not an escape from reality, not a hobby for "disinterested" neurotics in ivory towers, but the most crucial and practical power in human existence. Then let him become an intellectual leader who assumes full responsibility for the practical consequences of his theories.

The best among the businessmen should consider the function of wealth, and realize that the power behind the incomprehensible evil now unleashed against them is their own. Wealth, as such, is only a tool; by renouncing his intellect, the businessman has placed his wealth in the service of his own destroyers. They do not need to nationalize his property: they nationalized his mind long ago. Let him now realize that practical action without a theoretical base achieves the opposite of his goals, and that intellectual irresponsibility is not a way of escape from his enemies. Then let him discover the function of philosophy.

Instead of those ludicrous programs of "student exchanges" between America and Soviet Russia, for the alleged purpose of "gaining mutual understanding," there ought to be a private, voluntary program of "student exchanges" between the intellectuals and the businessmen, the two groups that need each other most, yet know less and understand less about each other than about any alien society in any distant corner of the globe. The businessmen need to discover the intellect; the intellectuals need to discover reality. Let the intellectuals understand the nature and the function of a free market in order to offer the businessmen, as well as the public at large, the guidance of an intelligible theoretical framework for dealing with men, with society, with politics, with economics. Let the businessmen learn the basic issues and principles of philosophy in order to know how to judge ideas, then let them assume full responsibility for the kind of ideologies they choose to finance and support.

Let them both discover the nature, the theory and the actual history of capitalism; both groups are equally ignorant of it. No other subject is hidden by so many distortions, misconceptions, misrepresentations and falsifications. Let them study the historical facts and discover that all the evils popularly ascribed to capitalism were caused, necessitated and made possible *only* by government controls imposed on the economy. Whenever they hear capitalism being denounced, let them check the facts and discover which of the two opposite political principles—free trade or government controls—was responsible for the alleged iniquities. When they hear it said that capitalism has had its chance and has failed, let them remember that what ultimately failed was a "mixed" economy, that the controls were the cause of the failure, and that the way to save a country is not by making it swallow a full, "unmixed" glass of the poison which is killing it.

The Founding Fathers were America's first intellectuals and, so far, her last. It is their basic political line that the New Intellectuals have to continue. Today, that line is lost under layer upon layer of evasions, equivocations and plain falsehood; today's Witch Doctors claim that the basic premise of the Founding Fathers was faith and uncritical compliance with tradition; today's Attila-ists claim that that basic premise was the subordination of the individual to the collective and his sacrifice to the public good. The New Intellectuals must remind the world that the basic premise of the Founding Fathers was man's right to his own life, to his own liberty, to the pursuit of his own happiness—which means: man's right to exist for his own sake, neither sacrificing himself to others nor sacrificing others to himself; and that the political implementation of this right is a society where men deal with one another as *traders*, by voluntary exchange to mutual benefit.

The moral premises *implicit* in the political philosophy of the Founding Fathers, in the social system they established and in the economics of capitalism, must now be recognized and accepted in the form of an *explicit* moral philosophy. That which is merely implicit is not in men's conscious control; they can lose it by means of other implications, without knowing what it is that they are losing or when or why. It was the morality of altruism that undercut America and is now destroying her. From her start, America was torn by the clash of her political system with the altruist morality. Capitalism and altruism are incompatible; they are philosophical opposites; they cannot co-exist in the same man or in the same society. Today, the conflict has reached its ultimate climax; the choice is clear-cut: either a new morality of rational self-interest, with its consequences of freedom, justice, progress and man's happiness on earth—or the primordial morality of altruism, with its consequences of slavery, brute force, stagnant terror and sacrificial furnaces.

The world crisis of today is a *moral* crisis—and nothing less than a moral revolution can resolve it: a moral revolution to sanction and complete the political achievement of the American Revolution. Evasions, equivocations and guilty apologies will not work any longer. The disgraceful injustice which penalized virtue for being virtue, which forced businessmen to apologize for their ability, for their success, for their achievements, has now been projected onto a global scale and translated into the disgraceful spectacle of America apologizing for her virtues and greatness to that bloody slaughterhouse of embodied altruism which is Soviet Russia.

The New Intellectuals must fight for capitalism, not as a "practical" issue, not as an economic issue, but, with the most righteous pride, as a *moral* issue. That is what capitalism deserves, and nothing less will save it.

The New Intellectuals must assume the task of building a new culture on a new moral foundation, which, for once, will not be the culture of Attila and the Witch Doctor, but the culture of the Producer. They will have to be *radicals* in the literal and reputable sense of the word: "radical" means "fundamental." The representatives of intellectual orthodoxy, conventionality and *status quo*, the Babbitts of today, are the collectivists. Let those who do care about the future, those willing to crusade for a perfect society, realize that the new *radicals* are the fighters for capitalism.

It is not an easy task and it cannot be achieved overnight. But the New Intellectuals have an inestimable advantage: they have reality on their side. The difficulties they will encounter on their way are not stone barriers, but fog: the heavy fog of passive disintegration, through which it will be hard for them to find one another. They will encounter no opposition, since, in this context, an opposition would have to possess *intellectual* weapons. As to their enemies, they should comply with their enemies' request—and leave them to heaven.

The process of identifying, judging, accepting and upholding a new philosophy of life is a long, complicated process, which requires thought, proof, full understanding and conviction. But there are two principles on which all men of intellectual integrity and good will can agree, as a "basic minimum," as a precondition of any discussion, co-operation or movement toward an intellectual Renaissance. One principle is epistemological, the other is moral; they are not axioms, but until a man has proved them to himself and has accepted them, he is not fit for an intellectual discussion. These two principles are: *a.* that emotions are not tools of cognition; *b.* that no man has the right to *initiate* the use of physical force against others.

a. The first of these two principles represents one's basic rejection of the Witch Doctor's psycho-epistemology. It means that one must differentiate between one's thoughts and one's emotions with full clarity and precision. One does not have to be omniscient in order to possess knowledge; one merely has to know that which one does know, and distinguish it from that which one feels. Nor does one need a full system of philosophical epistemology in order to distinguish one's own considered judgment from one's feelings, wishes, hopes or fears. Those who claim that they cannot do it are merely confessing that they have never learned how to use their mind and are incapable of perceiving, judging or evaluating reality. This may be a psychological problem, but it becomes an intellectual fraud when such persons enter a philosophical discussion and demand consideration for their ideas. No discussion, co-operation, agreement or understanding is possible among men who substitute emotion for proof.

b. This second principle represents one's basic rejection of Attila's psycho-epistemology. To claim the right to *initiate* the use of physical force against another man—the right to compel his agreement by the threat of physical destruction—is to evict oneself automatically from the realm of rights, of morality and of the intellect. Perhaps the most obscene legacy of altruism among modern intellectuals is their axiomatic acceptance of brute force and of somebody's sacrifice as a normal and necessary part of a human society, and their refusal to consider the possibility of a non-sacrificial, non-compulsory co-existence and co-operation among men. Observe that they cannot conceive of "selfishness" except in terms of sacrificing others to oneself, and they cannot conceive of anyone who does *not* regard such sacrificing as to his own interest. This, of course, is a psychological confession about the nature of their own desires and about the Attila in their souls. When they declare that they see no difference between economic power and political power—which means: no difference between an employer and a holdup man, no difference between the United States and Soviet Russia—they are confessing a Witch Doctor's abject fear of reality, which makes them equate a Producer with an Attila.

One would suppose that any man who makes claim to the title of moralist, humanitarian or intellectual would spend his life trying to devise—as an ideal—a social system where no man or group of men may initiate the use of physical force against others or demand the sacrifice of anyone to anyone. But when one remembers that such a system *was* devised and *did* exist less than a hundred years ago, one knows how to evaluate the brutes and thugs of the spirit who refuse to consider it possible.*

So long as men believe that the *initiation* of physical force by some men against others is a proper part of an organized society—hatred, violence, brutality, destruction, slaughter and the savage gang warfare of group against group are all they can or will achieve. When physical force is the ultimate arbiter, men are driven to connive, conspire and gang up on one another in order to destroy rather than be destroyed; the best perish, but the Attilas rise to the top. It might be understandable that primitive, savage tribes could not conceive of a way of life without resort to physical violence—and the bloody chaos of tribal warfare was all they achieved, as those who remained on that level still demonstrate today. But when men propose to live in an industrial civilization by the moral concepts of those jungle savages, with nuclear missiles and H-bombs at their disposal—they deserve the catastrophes they ask for. Let no man posture as an advocate of peace if he proposes or supports any social system that initiates the use of physical force against individual men, in any

---

* The epistemological chaos of today makes it necessary to stress that men have the right and the moral obligation of self-defense, that is: the right to use physical force only as retaliation and only against those who initiate its use. For a detailed discussion, see Galt's speech.

form whatever. Let no man posture as an advocate of freedom if he claims the right to establish *his* version of a good
society where individual dissenters are to be suppressed by
means of physical force. Let no man posture as an intellectual
if he proposes to elevate a thug into the position of final
authority over the intellect—or if he equates the power of
physical compulsion with the power of persuasion—or if he
equates the power of muscles with the power of ideas.

No advocate of reason can claim the right to force his
ideas on others. No advocate of the free mind can claim
the right to force the minds of others. No rational society,
no co-operation, no agreement, no understanding, no discussion are possible among men who propose to substitute
guns for rational persuasion.

If men of good will wish to come together for the purpose
of upholding reason and establishing a rational society, they
should begin by following the example of the cowboys in
Western movies when the sheriff tells them at the door to a
conference room: "Gentlemen, leave your guns outside."

Those who will accept the "basic minimum" of civilization,
the two principles stated above, will have made the first step
toward the building of a new culture in the wide-open spaces
of today's intellectual vacuum. There is an ancient slogan that
applies to our present position: "The king is dead—long live
the king!" We can say, with the same dedication to the future: "The intellectuals are dead—long live the intellectuals!"
—and then proceed to fulfill the responsibility which that
honorable title had once implied.

We the Living

This novel was published in 1936 and reissued in 1959. Its theme is: the individual against the state; the supreme value of a human life and the evil of the totalitarian state that claims the right to sacrifice it. The story takes place in Soviet Russia. The excerpt below is the speech of Kira Argounova to Andrei Taganov, in the following context: Kira has been having a love affair with Andrei in order to obtain money to save the life of Leo Kovalensky, the man she loves; Andrei, an idealistic young Communist, who is profoundly in love with her, was beginning to discover the importance of personal values, when, in the course of arresting Leo for a political crime, he learns the truth about Kira's relationship to both of them.

"No, you didn't know. But it was very simple. And not very unusual. Go through the garrets and basements where men live in your Red cities and see how many cases like this you can find. He wanted to live. You think everything that breathes can live? You've learned differently, I know. But he was one who could have lived. There aren't many of them, so they don't count with you. The doctor said he was going to die. And I loved him. You've learned what that means, too, haven't you? He didn't need much. Only rest, and fresh air, and food. He had no right to that, had he? Your State said so. We tried to beg. We begged humbly. Do you know what they said? There was a doctor in a hospital and he said he had hundreds on his waiting list....

"You see, you must understand this thoroughly. No one does. No one sees it, but I do, I can't help it, I see it, you must see it, too. You understand? Hundreds. Thousands. Millions. Millions of what? Stomachs, and heads, and legs, and

tongues, and souls. And it doesn't even matter whether they
fit together. Just millions. Just flesh. Human flesh. And they
—it—had been registered and numbered, you know, like tin
cans on a store shelf. I wonder if they're registered by the
person or by the pound? And they had a chance to go on living. But not Leo. He was only a man. All stones are cobble-
stones to you. And diamonds—they're useless, because they
sparkle too brightly in the sun, and it's too hard on the eyes,
and it's too hard under the hoofs marching into the proletarian future. You don't pave roads with diamonds. They may
have other uses in the world, but of those you've never
learned. That is why you had sentenced him to death, and
others like him, an execution without a firing squad. There
was a big commissar and I went to see him. He told me that a
hundred thousand workers had died in the civil war and why
couldn't one aristocrat die—in the face of the Union of Socialist Soviet Republics? And what is the Union of Socialist Soviet
Republics in the face of one man? But that is a question
not for you to answer. I'm grateful to that commissar. He
gave me permission to do what I've done. I don't hate him.
You should hate him. What I'm doing to you—he did it
first! . . .

"That's the question, you know, don't you? Why can't one
aristocrat die in the face of the Union of Socialist Soviet Republics? You don't understand that, do you? You and your
great commissar, and a million others, like you, like him,
that's what you brought to the world, that question and your
answer to it! A great gift, isn't it? But one of you has been
paid. I paid it. In you and to you. For all the sorrow your
comrades brought to a living world. How do you like it,
Comrade Andrei Taganov of the All-Union Communist Par-
ty? If you taught us that our life is nothing before that of
the State—well then, are you really suffering? If I brought
you to the last hell of despair—well then, why don't you
say that one's own life doesn't really matter? . . . You loved a
woman and she threw your love in your face? But the proletarian mines in the Don Basin have produced a hundred tons
of coal last month! You had two altars and you saw suddenly that a harlot stood on one of them, and Citizen Morozov
on the other? But the Proletarian State has exported ten thousand bushels of wheat last month! You've had every beam
knocked from under your life? But the Proletarian Republic is
building a new electric plant on the Volga! Why don't you

smile and sing hymns to the toil of the Collective? It's still there, your Collective. Go and join it. Did anything really happen to you? It's nothing but a personal problem of a private life, the kind that only the dead old world could worry about, isn't it? Don't you have something greater— greater is the word your comrades use—left to live for? Or do you, Comrade Taganov? . . .

"Now look at me! Take a good look! I was born and I knew I was alive and I knew what I wanted. What do you think is alive in me? Why do you think I'm alive? Because I have a stomach and eat and digest the food? Because I breathe and work and produce more food to digest? Or because I know what I want, and that something which knows how to want—isn't that life itself? And who—in this damned universe—who can tell me why I should live for anything but for that which I want? Who can answer that in human sounds that speak for human reason? . . . But you've tried to tell us what we should want. You came as a solemn army to bring a new life to men. You tore that life you knew nothing about, out of their guts—and you told them what it had to be. You took their every hour, every minute, every nerve, every thought in the farthest corners of their souls—and you told them what it had to be. You came and you forbade life to the living. You've driven us all into an iron cellar and you've closed all doors, and you've locked us airtight, airtight till the blood vessels of our spirits burst! Then you stare and wonder what it's doing to us. Well, then, look! All of you who have eyes left—look!"

Anthem

This novelette was first published in England in 1938. Its theme is: the meaning of man's ego. It projects a society of the future, which has accepted total collectivism with all of its ultimate consequences: men have relapsed into primitive savagery and stagnation; the word "I" has vanished from the human language, there are no singular pronouns, a man refers to himself as "we" and to another man as "they." The story presents the gradual rediscovery of the word "I" by a man of intransigent mind. The following excerpt is from his statement about his discovery.

"I am. I think. I will. . . .

"What must I say besides? These are the words. This is the answer.

"I stand here on the summit of the mountain. I lift my head and I spread my arms. This—my body and spirit—this is the end of the quest. I wished to know the meaning of things. I am the meaning. I wished to find a warrant for being. I need no warrant for being, and no word of sanction upon my being. I am the warrant and the sanction. . . .

"I know not if this earth on which I stand is the core of the universe or if it is but a speck of dust lost in eternity. I know not and I care not. For I know what happiness is possible to me on earth. And my happiness needs no higher aim to vindicate it. My happiness is not the means to any end. It is the end. It is its own goal. It is its own purpose.

"Neither am I the means to any end others may wish to accomplish. I am not a tool for their use. I am not a servant of their needs. I am not a bandage for their wounds. I am not a sacrifice on their altars. . . .

"I owe nothing to my brothers, nor do I gather debts from

them. I ask none to live for me, nor do I live for any others. I covet no man's soul, nor is my soul theirs to covet.

"I am neither foe nor friend to my brothers, but such as each of them shall deserve of me. And to earn my love, my brothers must do more than to have been born. I do not grant my love without reason, nor to any chance passer-by who may wish to claim it. I honor men with my love. But honor is a thing to be earned.

"I shall choose friends among men, but neither slaves nor masters. And I shall choose only such as please me, and them I shall love and respect, but neither command nor obey. And we shall join our hands when we wish, or walk alone when we so desire. For in the temple of his spirit, each man is alone. Let each man keep his temple untouched and undefiled. Then let him join hands with others if he wishes, but only beyond his holy threshold.

"For the word 'We' must never be spoken, save by one's choice and as a second thought. This word must never be placed first within man's soul, else it becomes a monster, the root of all the evils on earth, the root of man's torture by men, and of an unspeakable lie.

"The word 'We' is as lime poured over men, which sets and hardens to stone, and crushes all beneath it, and that which is white and that which is black are lost equally in the gray of it. It is the word by which the depraved steal the virtue of the good, by which the weak steal the might of the strong, by which the fools steal the wisdom of the sages.

"What is my joy if all hands, even the unclean, can reach into it? What is my wisdom, if even the fools can dictate to me? What is my freedom, if all creatures, even the botched and the impotent, are my masters? What is my life, if I am but to bow, to agree and to obey?

"But I am done with this creed of corruption.

"I am done with the monster of 'We,' the word of serfdom, of plunder, of misery, falsehood and shame.

"And now I see the face of god, and I raise this god over the earth, this god whom men have sought since men came into being, this god who will grant them joy and peace and pride.

"This god, this one word: **I**."

The Fountainhead

This novel was published in 1943. Its theme is: individualism versus collectivism, not in politics, but in man's soul; the psychological motivations and the basic premises that produce the character of an individualist or a collectivist. The story presents the career of Howard Roark, an architect and innovator, who breaks with tradition, recognizes no authority but that of his own independent judgment, struggles for the integrity of his creative work against every form of social opposition—and wins.

THE NATURE OF THE SECOND-HANDER

This excerpt is from a conversation between Roark and his friend Gail Wynand, in which Roark explains what he has discovered about the psychology of those whose basic motivation is the opposite of his own.

"It's what I couldn't understand about people for a long time. They have no self. They live within others. They live second-hand. Look at Peter Keating. . . . I've looked at him—at what's left of him—and it's helped me to understand. He's paying the price and wondering for what sin and telling himself that he's been too selfish. In what act or thought of his has there ever been a self? What was his aim in life? Greatness—in other people's eyes. Fame, admiration, envy—all that which comes from others. Others dictated his convictions, which he did not hold, but he was satisfied that others believed he held them. Others were his motive power and his prime concern. He didn't want to be great, but to be thought great.

He didn't want to build, but to be admired as a builder. He borrowed from others in order to make an impression on others. There's your actual selflessness. It's his ego that he's betrayed and given up. But everybody calls him selfish. . . .

"Isn't that the root of every despicable action? Not selfishness, but precisely the absence of a self. Look at them. The man who cheats and lies, but preserves a respectable front. He knows himself to be dishonest, but others think he's honest and he derives his self-respect from that, second-hand. The man who takes credit for an achievement which is not his own. He knows himself to be mediocre, but he's great in the eyes of others. The frustrated wretch who professes love for the inferior and clings to those less endowed, in order to establish his own superiority by comparison. . . . They're second-handers. . . .

"They have no concern for facts, ideas, work. They're concerned only with people. They don't ask: 'Is this true?' They ask: 'Is this what others think is true?' Not to judge, but to repeat. Not to do, but to give the impression of doing. Not creation, but show. Not ability, but friendship. Not merit, but pull. What would happen to the world without those who do, think, work, produce? Those are the egoists. You don't think through another's brain and you don't work through another's hands. When you suspend your faculty of independent judgment, you suspend consciousness. To stop consciousness is to stop life. Second-handers have no sense of reality. Their reality is not within them, but somewhere in that space which divides one human body from another. Not an entity, but a relation—anchored to nothing. That's the emptiness I couldn't understand in people. That's what stopped me whenever I faced a committee. Men without an ego. Opinion without a rational process. Motion without brakes or motor. Power without responsibility. The second-hander acts, but the source of his actions is scattered in every other living person. It's everywhere and nowhere and you can't reason with him. He's not open to reason. You can't speak to him—he can't hear. You're tried by an empty bench. A blind mass running amuck, to crush you without sense or purpose. . . ."

"Notice how they'll accept anything except a man who stands alone. They recognize him at once. . . . There's a special, insidious kind of hatred for him. They forgive criminals.

They admire dictators. Crime and violence are a tie. A form of mutual dependence. They need ties. They've got to force their miserable little personalities on every single person they meet. The independent man kills them—because they don't exist within him and that's the only form of existence they know. Notice the malignant kind of resentment against any idea that propounds independence. Notice the malice toward an independent man...."

"After centuries of being pounded with the doctrine that altruism is the ultimate ideal, men have accepted it in the only way it could be accepted. By seeking self-esteem through others. By living second-hand. And it has opened the way for every kind of horror. It has become the dreadful form of selfishness which a truly selfish man couldn't have conceived. And now, to cure a world perishing from selflessness, we're asked to destroy the self. Listen to what is being preached today. Look at everyone around us. You've wondered why they suffer, why they seek happiness and never find it. If any man stopped and asked himself whether he's ever held a truly personal desire, he'd find the answer. He'd see that all his wishes, his efforts, his dreams, his ambitions are motivated by other men. He's not really struggling even for material wealth, but for the second-hander's delusion—prestige. A stamp of approval, not his own. He can find no joy in the struggle and no joy when he has succeeded. He can't say about a single thing: 'This is what I wanted because *I* wanted it, not because it made my neighbors gape at me.' Then he wonders why he's unhappy. Every form of happiness is private. Our greatest moments are personal, self-motivated, not to be touched. The things which are sacred or precious to us are the things we withdraw from promiscuous sharing. But now we are taught to throw everything within us into public light and common pawing. To seek joy in meeting halls. We haven't even got a word for the quality I mean—for the self-sufficiency of man's spirit. It's difficult to call it selfishness or egoism, the words have been perverted, they've come to mean Peter Keating. Gail, I think the only cardinal evil on earth is that of placing your prime concern within other men. I've always demanded a certain quality in the people I liked. I've always recognized it at once—and it's the only quality I respect in men. I chose my friends by that. Now I know what it is. A self-sufficient ego. Nothing else matters."

THE SOUL OF A COLLECTIVIST

This excerpt is the confession of Roark's antipode and arch-enemy, Ellsworth M. Toohey, an architectural critic and sociologist, who spends his life plotting the future establishment of a collectivist society. He is addressing one of his own victims.

"I've always said just that. Clearly, precisely and openly. It's not my fault if you couldn't hear. You could, of course. You didn't want to. Which was safer than deafness—for me. I said I intended to rule. Like all my spiritual predecessors. But I'm luckier than they were. I inherited the fruit of their efforts and I shall be the one who'll see the great dream made real. I see it all around me today. I recognize it. I don't like it. I didn't expect to like it. Enjoyment is not my destiny. I shall find such satisfaction as my capacity permits. I shall rule. . . .

"It's only a matter of discovering the lever. If you learn how to rule one single man's soul, you can get the rest of mankind. It's the soul, Peter, the soul. Not whips or swords or fire or guns. That's why the Caesars, the Attilas, the Napoleons were fools and did not last. We will. The soul, Peter, is that which can't be ruled. It must be broken. Drive a wedge in, get your fingers on it—and the man is yours. You won't need a whip—he'll bring it to you and ask to be whipped. Set him in reverse—and his own mechanism will do your work for you. Use him against himself. Want to know how it's done? See if I ever lied to you. See if you haven't heard all this for years, but didn't want to hear, and the fault is yours, not mine. There are many ways. Here's one. Make man feel small. Make him feel guilty. Kill his aspiration and his integrity. That's difficult. The worst among you gropes for an ideal in his own twisted way. Kill integrity by internal corruption. Use it against itself. Direct it toward a goal destructive of all integrity. Preach selflessness. Tell man that he must live for others. Tell men that altruism is the ideal.

Not a single one of them has ever achieved it and not a single one ever will. His every living instinct screams against it. But don't you see what you accomplish? Man realizes that he's incapable of what he's accepted as the noblest virtue—and it gives him a sense of guilt, of sin, of his own basic unworthiness. Since the supreme ideal is beyond his grasp he gives up eventually all ideals, all aspiration, all sense of his personal value. He feels himself obliged to preach what he can't practice. But one can't be good halfway or honest approximately. To preserve one's integrity is a hard battle. Why preserve that which one knows to be corrupt already? His soul gives up its self-respect. You've got him. He'll obey. He'll be glad to obey—because he can't trust himself, he feels uncertain, he feels unclean. That's one way. Here's another. Kill man's sense of values. Kill his capacity to recognize greatness or to achieve it. Great men can't be ruled. We don't want any great men. Don't deny the conception of greatness. Destroy it from within. The great is the rare, the difficult, the exceptional. Set up standards of achievement open to all, to the least, to the most inept—and you stop the impetus to effort in all men, great or small. You stop all incentive to improvement, to excellence, to perfection. . . . Don't set out to raze all shrines—you'll frighten men. Enshrine mediocrity—and the shrines are razed. Then there's another way. Kill by laughter. Laughter is an instrument of human joy. Learn to use it as a weapon of destruction. Turn it into a sneer. It's simple. Tell them to laugh at everything. Tell them that a sense of humor is an unlimited virtue. Don't let anything remain sacred in a man's soul—and his soul won't be sacred to him. Kill reverence and you've killed the hero in man. One doesn't reverence with a giggle. He'll obey and he'll set no limits to his obedience—anything goes—nothing is too serious. Here's another way. This is most important. Don't allow men to be happy. Happiness is self-contained and self-sufficient. Happy men have no time and no use for you. Happy men are free men. So kill their joy in living. Take away from them whatever is dear or important to them. Never let them have what they want. Make them feel that the mere fact of a personal desire is evil. Bring them to a state where saying 'I want' is no longer a natural right, but a shameful admission. Altruism is of great help in this. Unhappy men will come to you. They'll need you. They'll come for consolation, for support, for escape.

Nature allows no vacuum. Empty man's soul—and the space is yours to fill. I don't see why you should look so shocked, Peter. This is the oldest one of all. Look back at history. Look at any great system of ethics, from the Orient up. Didn't they all preach the sacrifice of personal joy? Under all the complications of verbiage, haven't they all had a single leitmotif: sacrifice, renunciation, self-denial? Haven't you been able to catch their theme song—'Give up, give up, give up, give up'? Look at the moral atmosphere of today. Everything enjoyable, from cigarettes to sex to ambition to the profit motive, is considered depraved or sinful. Just prove that a thing makes men happy—and you've damned it. That's how far we've come. We've tied happiness to guilt. And we've got mankind by the throat. Throw your first-born into a sacrificial furnace—lie on a bed of nails—go into the desert to mortify the flesh—don't dance—don't go to the movies on Sunday—don't try to get rich—don't smoke— don't drink. It's all the same line. The great line. Fools think that taboos of this nature are just nonsense. Something left over, old-fashioned. But there's always a purpose in nonsense. Don't bother to examine a folly—ask yourself only what it accomplishes. Every system of ethics that preached sacrifice grew into a world power and ruled millions of men. Of course, you must dress it up. You must tell people that they'll achieve a superior kind of happiness by giving up everything that makes them happy. You don't have to be too clear about it. Use big vague words. 'Universal Harmony' —'Eternal Spirit'—'Divine Purpose'—'Nirvana'—'Paradise'— 'Racial Supremacy'—'The Dictatorship of the Proletariat.' In- ternal corruption, Peter. That's the oldest one of all. The farce has been going on for centuries and men still fall for it. Yet the test should be so simple: just listen to any prophet and if you hear him speak of sacrifice—run. Run faster than from a plague. It stands to reason that where there's sacrifice, there's someone collecting sacrificial offer- ings. Where there's service, there's someone being served. The man who speaks to you of sacrifice, speaks of slaves and masters. And intends to be the master. But if ever you hear a man telling you that you must be happy, that it's your natural right, that your first duty is to yourself—that will be the man who's not after your soul. That will be the man who has nothing to gain from you. But let him come and you'll scream your empty heads off, howling that he's a selfish monster. So the racket is safe for many, many centuries. But here you might have noticed something. I said, 'It stands to reason.' Do you see? Men have a weapon against you. Reason. So you must be very sure to take it away from them. Cut the props from under it. But be careful. Don't deny outright. Never deny anything outright, you give your hand away. Don't say reason is evil—though some have gone that far and with astonishing success. Just say that reason is limited. That there's something above it. What? You don't have to be too clear about it either. The field's inexhaustible. 'Instinct'—'Feeling'—'Revelation'—'Divine Intuition'—'Dialectical Materialism.' If you get caught at some crucial point and somebody tells you that your doctrine doesn't make sense—you're ready for him. You tell him that there's something above sense. That here he must not try to think, he must *feel*. He must *believe*. Suspend reason and you play it deuces wild. Anything goes in any manner you wish whenever you need it. You've got him. Can you rule a thinking man? We don't want any thinking men. . . .

"Peter, you've heard all this. You've seen me practicing it for ten years. You see it being practiced all over the world. Why are you disgusted? You have no right to sit there and stare at me with the virtuous superiority of being shocked. You're in on it. You've taken your share and you've got to go along. You're afraid to see where it's leading. I'm not. I'll tell you. The world of the future. The world I want. A world of obedience and unity. A world where the thought of each man will not be his own, but an attempt to guess the thought in the brain of his neighbor who'll have no thought of his own but an attempt to guess the thought of the next neighbor who'll have no thought—and so on, Peter, around the globe. Since all must agree with all. A world where no man will hold a desire for himself, but will direct all his efforts to satisfy the desires of his neighbor who'll have no desires except to satisfy the desires of the next neighbor who'll have no desires—around the globe, Peter. Since all must serve all. A world in which man will not work for so innocent an incentive as money, but for that headless monster —prestige. The approval of his fellows—their good opinion— the opinion of men who'll be allowed to hold no opinion. An octopus, all tentacles and no brain. Judgment, Peter? Not judgment, but public polls. An average drawn upon zeros —since no individuality will be permitted. A world with its motor cut off and a single heart, pumped by hand. My hand —and the hands of a few, a very few other men like me. Those who know what makes you tick—you great, wonderful average, you who have not risen in fury when we called you the average, the little, the common, you who've liked and accepted those names. You'll sit enthroned and enshrined, you, the little people, the absolute ruler to make all past rulers squirm with envy, the absolute, the unlimited, God and Prophet and King combined. *Vox populi*. The average, the common, the general. Do you know the proper antonym for Ego? Bromide, Peter. The rule of the bromide. But even the trite has to be originated by someone at some time. We'll do the originating. *Vox dei*. We'll enjoy unlimited submission—from men who've learned nothing except to submit. We'll call it 'to serve.' We'll give out medals for service. You'll fall over one another in a scramble to see who can submit better and more. There will be no other distinction to seek. No other form of personal achievement. Can you see Howard Roark in the picture? No? Then don't waste time on foolish questions. Everything that can't be ruled, must go. And if freaks persist in being born occasionally, they will not survive beyond their twelfth year. When their brain begins to function, it will feel the pressure and it will explode. The pressure gauged to a vacuum. Do you know the fate of deep-sea creatures brought out to sunlight? So much for future Roarks. The rest of you will smile and obey. Have you noticed that the imbecile always smiles? Man's first frown is the first touch of God on his forehead. The touch of thought. But we'll have neither God nor thought. Only voting by smiles. Automatic levers—all saying yes . . . Now if you were a little more intelligent— like your ex-wife, for instance—you'd ask: What of us, the rulers? What of me, Ellsworth Monkton Toohey? And I'd say, Yes, you're right. I'll achieve no more than you will. I'll have no purpose save to keep you contented. To lie, to flatter you, to praise you, to inflate your vanity. To make speeches about the people and the common good. Peter, my poor old friend, I'm the most selfless man you've ever known. I have less independence than you, whom I just forced to sell your soul. You've used people at least for the sake of what you could get from them for yourself. I want nothing for myself. I use people for the sake of what I can do to them. It's my only function and satisfaction. I have no private purpose. I want power. I want my world of the future. Let all live for all. Let all sacrifice and none profit. Let all suffer and none enjoy. Let progress stop. Let all stagnate. There's equality in stagnation. All subjugated to the will of all. Universal slavery—without even the dignity of a master. Slavery to slavery. A great circle—and a total equality. The world of the future. . . .

"Look around you. Pick up any newspaper and read the headlines. Isn't it coming? Isn't it here? Every single thing I told you? Isn't Europe swallowed already and we're stumbling on to follow? Everything I said is contained in a single word—collectivism. And isn't that the god of our century? To act together. To think—together. To feel—together. To unite, to agree, to obey. To obey, to serve, to sacrifice. Divide and conquer—first. But then—unite and rule. We've discovered that one at last. Remember the Roman Emperor who said he wished humanity had a single neck so he could cut it? People have laughed at him for centuries. But we'll have the last laugh. We've accomplished what he couldn't accomplish. We've taught men to unite. This makes one neck ready for one leash. We've found the magic word. Collectivism. Look at Europe, you fool. Can't you see past the guff and recognize the essence? One country is dedicated to the proposition that man has no rights, that the collective is all. The individual held as evil, the mass—as God. No motive and no virtue permitted—except that of service to the proletariat. That's one version. Here's another. A country dedicated to the proposition that man has no rights, that the State is all. The individual held as evil, the race—as God. No motive and no virtue permitted—except that of service to the race. Am I raving or is this the cold reality of two continents already? Watch the pincer movement. If you're sick of one version, we push you into the other. We get you coming and going. We've closed the doors. We've fixed the coin. Heads—collectivism, and tails—collectivism. Fight the doctrine which slaughters the individual with a doctrine which slaughters the individual. Give up your soul to a council—or give it up to a leader. But give it up, give it up, give it up. My technique, Peter. Offer poison as food and poison as antidote. Go fancy on the trimmings, but hang on to the main objective. Give the fools a choice, let them have their fun—but don't forget the only purpose you have to accomplish. Kill the individual. Kill man's soul. The rest will follow automatically."

THE SOUL OF AN INDIVIDUALIST

This is the speech that Howard Roark makes in his own defense, while on trial for having dynamited a government housing project under construction; he had designed the project for another architect, Peter Keating, on the agreement that it would be built exactly as he designed it; the agreement was broken by the government agency; the two architects had no recourse to law, not being permitted to sue the government.

"Thousands of years ago, the first man discovered how to make fire. He was probably burned at the stake he had taught his brothers to light. He was considered an evildoer who had dealt with a demon mankind dreaded. But thereafter men had fire to keep them warm, to cook their food, to light their caves. He had left them a gift they had not conceived and he had lifted darkness off the earth. Centuries later, the first man invented the wheel. He was probably torn on the rack he had taught his brothers to build. He was considered a transgressor who ventured into forbidden territory. But thereafter, men could travel past any horizon. He had left them a gift they had not conceived and he had opened the roads of the world.

"That man, the unsubmissive and first, stands in the opening chapter of every legend mankind has recorded about its beginning. Prometheus was chained to a rock and torn by vultures—because he had stolen the fire of the gods. Adam was condemned to suffer—because he had eaten the fruit of the tree of knowledge. Whatever the legend, somewhere in the shadows of its memory mankind knew that its glory began with one and that that one paid for his courage.

"Throughout the centuries there were men who took first steps down new roads armed with nothing but their own vision. Their goals differed, but they all had this in common: that the step was first, the road new, the vision unborrowed, and the response they received—hatred. The great creators —the thinkers, the artists, the scientists, the inventors—stood alone against the men of their time. Every great new thought was opposed. Every great new invention was denounced. The first motor was considered foolish. The airplane was considered impossible. The power loom was considered vicious. Anesthesia was considered sinful. But the men of unborrowed vision went ahead. They fought, they suffered and they paid. But they won.

"No creator was prompted by a desire to serve his brothers, for his brothers rejected the gift he offered and that gift destroyed the slothful routine of their lives. His truth was his only motive. His own truth, and his own work to achieve it in his own way. A symphony, a book, an engine, a philosophy, an airplane or a building—that was his goal and his life. Not those who heard, read, operated, believed, flew or inhabited the thing he had created. The creation, not its users. The creation, not the benefits others derived from it. The creation which gave form to his truth. He held his truth above all things and against all men.

"His vision, his strength, his courage came from his own spirit. A man's spirit, however, is his self. That entity which is his consciousness. To think, to feel, to judge, to act are functions of the ego.

"The creators were not selfless. It is the whole secret of their power—that it was self-sufficient, self-motivated, self-generated. A first cause, a fount of energy, a life force, a Prime Mover. The creator served nothing and no one. He lived for himself.

"And only by living for himself was he able to achieve the things which are the glory of mankind. Such is the nature of achievement.

"Man cannot survive except through his mind. He comes on earth unarmed. His brain is his only weapon. Animals obtain food by force. Man has no claws, no fangs, no horns, no great strength of muscle. He must plant his food or hunt it. To plant, he needs a process of thought. To hunt, he needs weapons, and to make weapons—a process of thought. From this simplest necessity to the highest religious abstraction, from the wheel to the skyscraper, everything we are and everything we have comes from a single attribute of man—the function of his reasoning mind.

"But the mind is an attribute of the individual. There is no such thing as a collective brain. There is no such thing as a collective thought. An agreement reached by a group of men is only a compromise or an average drawn upon many individual thoughts. It is a secondary consequence. The primary act—the process of reason—must be performed by each man alone. We can divide a meal among many men. We cannot digest it in a collective stomach. No man can use his lungs to breathe for another man. No man can use his brain to think for another. All the functions of body and spirit are private. They cannot be shared or transferred.

"We inherit the products of the thought of other men. We inherit the wheel. We make a cart. The cart becomes an automobile. The automobile becomes an airplane. But all through the process what we receive from others is only the end product of their thinking. The moving force is the creative faculty which takes this product as material, uses it and originates the next step. This creative faculty cannot be given or received, shared or borrowed. It belongs to single, individual men. That which it creates is the property of the creator. Men learn from one another. But all learning is only the exchange of material. No man can give another the capacity to think. Yet that capacity is our only means of survival.

"Nothing is given to man on earth. Everything he needs has to be produced. And here man faces his basic alternative: he can survive in only one of two ways—by the independent work of his own mind or as a parasite fed by the minds of others. The creator originates. The parasite borrows. The creator faces nature alone. The parasite faces nature through an intermediary.

"The creator's concern is the conquest of nature. The parasite's concern is the conquest of men.

"The creator lives for his work. He needs no other men. His primary goal is within himself. The parasite lives secondhand. He needs others. Others become his prime motive.

"The basic need of the creator is independence. The reasoning mind cannot work under any form of compulsion. It cannot be curbed, sacrificed or subordinated to any consideration whatsoever. It demands total independence in function and in motive. To a creator, all relations with men are secondary.

"The basic need of the second-hander is to secure his ties with men in order to be fed. He places relations first. He declares that man exists in order to serve others. He preaches altruism.

"Altruism is the doctrine which demands that man live for others and place others above self.

"No man can live for another. He cannot share his spirit just as he cannot share his body. But the second-hander has used altruism as a weapon of exploitation and reversed the base of mankind's moral principles. Men have been taught every precept that destroys the creator. Men have been taught dependence as a virtue.

"The man who attempts to live for others is a dependent. He is a parasite in motive and makes parasites of those he serves. The relationship produces nothing but mutual corruption. It is impossible in concept. The nearest approach to it in reality—the man who lives to serve others—is the slave. If physical slavery is repulsive, how much more repulsive is the concept of servility of the spirit? The conquered slave has a vestige of honor. He has the merit of having resisted and of considering his condition evil. But the man who enslaves himself voluntarily in the name of love is the basest of creatures. He degrades the dignity of man and he degrades the conception of love. But this is the essence of altruism.

"Men have been taught that the highest virtue is not to achieve, but to give. Yet one cannot give that which has not been created. Creation comes before distribution—or there will be nothing to distribute. The need of the creator comes before the need of any possible beneficiary. Yet we are taught to admire the second-hander who dispenses gifts he has not produced above the man who made the gifts possible. We praise an act of charity. We shrug at an act of achievement.

"Men have been taught that their first concern is to relieve the suffering of others. But suffering is a disease. Should one come upon it, one tries to give relief and assistance. To make that the highest test of virtue is to make suffering the most important part of life. Then man must wish to see others suffer—in order that he may be virtuous. Such is the nature of altruism. The creator is not concerned with disease, but with life. Yet the work of the creators has eliminated one form of disease after another, in man's body and spirit, and brought more relief from suffering than any altruist could ever conceive.

"Men have been taught that it is a virtue to agree with others. But the creator is the man who disagrees. Men have been taught that it is a virtue to swim with the current. But the creator is the man who goes against the current. Men have been taught that it is a virtue to stand together. But the creator is the man who stands alone.

"Men have been taught that the ego is the synonym of evil, and selflessness the ideal of virtue. But the creator is the egoist in the absolute sense, and the selfless man is the one who does not think, feel, judge or act. These are functions of the self.

"Here the basic reversal is most deadly. The issue has been perverted and man has been left no alternative—and no freedom. As poles of good and evil, he was offered two conceptions: egoism and altruism. Egoism was held to mean the sacrifice of others to self. Altruism—the sacrifice of self to others. This tied man irrevocably to other men and left him nothing but a choice of pain: his own pain borne for the sake of others or pain inflicted upon others for the sake of self. When it was added that man must find joy in self-immolation, the trap was closed. Man was forced to accept masochism as his ideal—under the threat that sadism was his only alternative. This was the greatest fraud ever perpetrated on mankind.

"This was the device by which dependence and suffering were perpetuated as fundamentals of life.

"The choice is not self-sacrifice or domination. The choice is independence or dependence. The code of the creator or the code of the second-hander. This is the basic issue. It rests upon the alternative of life or death. The code of the creator is built on the needs of the reasoning mind which allows man to survive. The code of the second-hander is built on the needs of a mind incapable of survival. All that which proceeds from man's independent ego is good. All that which proceeds from man's dependence upon men is evil.

"The egoist in the absolute sense is not the man who sacrifices others. He is the man who stands above the need of using others in any manner. He does not function through them. He is not concerned with them in any primary matter. Not in his aim, not in his motive, not in his thinking, not in his desires, not in the source of his energy. He does not exist for any other man—and he asks no other man to exist for him. This is the only form of brotherhood and mutual respect possible between men.

"Degrees of ability vary, but the basic principle remains the same: the degree of a man's independence, initiative and personal love for his work determines his talent as a worker and his worth as a man. Independence is the only gauge of human virtue and value. What a man is and makes of himself; not what he has or hasn't done for others. There is no substitute for personal dignity. There is no standard of personal dignity except independence.

"In all proper relationships there is no sacrifice of anyone to anyone. An architect needs clients, but he does not subordinate his work to their wishes. They need him, but they do not order a house just to give him a commission. Men exchange their work by free, mutual consent to mutual advantage when their personal interests agree and they both desire the exchange. If they do not desire it, they are not forced to deal with each other. They seek further. This is the only possible form of relationship between equals. Anything else is a relation of slave to master, or victim to executioner.

"No work is ever done collectively, by a majority decision. Every creative job is achieved under the guidance of a single individual thought. An architect requires a great many men to erect his building. But he does not ask them to vote on his design. They work together by free agreement and each is free in his proper function. An architect uses steel, glass, concrete, produced by others. But the materials remain just so much steel, glass and concrete until he touches them. What he does with them is his individual product and his individual property. This is the only pattern for proper co-operation among men.

"The first right on earth is the right of the ego. Man's first duty is to himself. His moral law is never to place his prime goal within the persons of others. His moral obligation is to do what he wishes, provided his wish does not depend *primarily* upon other men. This includes the whole sphere of his creative faculty, his thinking, his work. But it does not include the sphere of the gangster, the altruist and the dictator.

"A man thinks and works alone. A man cannot rob, exploit or rule—alone. Robbery, exploitation and ruling presuppose victims. They imply dependence. They are the province of the second-hander.

"Rulers of men are not egoists. They create nothing. They exist entirely through the persons of others. Their goal is in their subjects, in the activity of enslaving. They are as dependent as the beggar, the social worker and the bandit. The form of dependence does not matter.

"But men were taught to regard second-handers—tyrants, emperors, dictators—as exponents of egoism. By this fraud they were made to destroy the ego, themselves and others. The purpose of the fraud was to destroy the creators. Or to harness them. Which is a synonym.

"From the beginning of history, the two antagonists have stood face to face: the creator and the second-hander. When the first creator invented the wheel, the first second-hander responded. He invented altruism.

"The creator—denied, opposed, persecuted, exploited—went on, moved forward and carried all humanity along on his energy. The second-hander contributed nothing to the process except the impediments. The contest has another name: the individual against the collective.

"The 'common good' of a collective—a race, a class, a state—was the claim and justification of every tyranny ever established over men. Every major horror of history was committed in the name of an altruistic motive. Has any act of selfishness ever equaled the carnage perpetrated by disciples of altruism? Does the fault lie in men's hypocrisy or in the nature of the principle? The most dreadful butchers were the most sincere. They believed in the perfect society reached through the guillotine and the firing squad. Nobody questioned their right to murder since they were murdering for an altruistic purpose. It was accepted that man must be sacrificed for other men. Actors change, but the course of the tragedy remains the same. A humanitarian who starts with declarations of love for mankind and ends with a sea of blood. It goes on and will go on so long as men believe that an action is good if it is unselfish. That permits the altruist to act and forces his victims to bear it. The leaders of collectivist movements ask nothing for themselves. But observe the results.

"The only good which men can do to one another and the only statement of their proper relationship is—Hands off!

"Now observe the results of a society built on the principle of individualism. This, our country. The noblest country in the history of men. The country of greatest achievement, greatest prosperity, greatest freedom. This country was not based on selfless service, sacrifice, renunciation or any precept of altruism. It was based on a man's right to the pursuit of happiness. His own happiness. Not anyone else's. A private, personal, selfish motive. Look at the results. Look into your own conscience.

"It is an ancient conflict. Men have come close to the truth, but it was destroyed each time and one civilization fell after another. Civilization is the progress toward a society of privacy. The savage's whole existence is public, ruled by the laws of his tribe. Civilization is the process of setting man free from men.

"Now, in our age, collectivism, the rule of the second-hander and second-rater, the ancient monster, has broken loose and is running amuck. It has brought men to a level of intellectual indecency never equaled on earth. It has reached a scale of horror without precedent. It has poisoned every mind. It has swallowed most of Europe. It is engulfing our country.

"I am an architect. I know what is to come by the principle on which it is built. We are approaching a world in which I cannot permit myself to live.

"Now you know why I dynamited Cortlandt.

"I designed Cortlandt. I gave it to you. I destroyed it.

"I destroyed it because I did not choose to let it exist. It was a double monster. In form and in implication. I had to blast both. The form was mutilated by two second-handers who assumed the right to improve upon that which they had not made and could not equal. They were permitted to do it by the general implication that the altruistic purpose of the building superseded all rights and that I had no claim to stand against it.

"I agreed to design Cortlandt for the purpose of seeing it erected as I designed it and for no other reason. That was the price I set for my work. I was not paid.

"I do not blame Peter Keating. He was helpless. He had a contract with his employers. It was ignored. He had a promise that the structure he offered would be built as designed. The promise was broken. The love of a man for the integrity of his work and his right to preserve it are now considered a vague intangible and an inessential. You have heard the prosecutor say that. Why was the building disfigured? For no reason. Such acts never have any reason, unless it's the vanity of some second-handers who feel they have a right to anyone's property, spiritual or material. Who permitted them to do it? No particular man among the dozens in authority. No one cared to permit or to stop it. No one was responsible. No one can be held to account. Such is the nature of all collective action.

"I did not receive the payment I asked. But the owners of Cortlandt got what they needed from me. They wanted a scheme devised to build a structure as cheaply as possible. They found no one else who could do it to their satisfaction. I could and did. They took the benefit of my work and made me contribute it as a gift. But I am not an altruist. I do not contribute gifts of this nature.

"It is said that I have destroyed the home of the destitute. It is forgotten that but for me the destitute could not have had this particular home. Those who were concerned with the poor had to come to me, who have never been concerned, in order to help the poor. It is believed that the poverty of the future tenants gave them a right to my work. That their need constituted a claim on my life. That it was my duty to contribute anything demanded of me. This is the second-hander's credo now swallowing the world.

"I came here to say that I do not recognize anyone's right to one minute of my life. Nor to any part of my energy. Nor to any achievement of mine. No matter who makes the claim, how large their number or how great their need.

"I wished to come here and say that I am a man who does not exist for others.

"It had to be said. The world is perishing from an orgy of self-sacrificing.

"I wished to come here and say that the integrity of a man's creative work is of greater importance than any charitable endeavor. Those of you who do not understand this are the men who're destroying the world.

"I wished to come here and state my terms. I do not care to exist on any others.

"I recognize no obligations toward men except one: to respect their freedom and to take no part in a slave society. To my country, I wish to give the ten years which I will spend in jail if my country exists no longer. I will spend them in memory and in gratitude for what my country has been. It will be my act of loyalty, my refusal to live or work in what has taken its place.

"My act of loyalty to every creator who ever lived and was made to suffer by the force responsible for the Cortlandt I dynamited. To every tortured hour of loneliness, denial, frustration, abuse he was made to spend—and to the battles he won. To every creator whose name is known—and to every creator who lived, struggled and perished unrecognized before he could achieve. To every creator who was destroyed in body or in spirit. To Henry Cameron. To Steven Mallory. To a man who doesn't want to be named, but who is sitting in this courtroom and knows that I am speaking of him."

Atlas Shrugged

This novel was published in 1957. Its theme is: the role of the mind in man's existence—and, as corollary, the demonstration of a new moral philosophy: the morality of rational self-interest.

The story shows what happens to the world when the mind goes on strike—when the men of creative ability, in every profession, quit and disappear. To quote John Galt, the leader and initiator of the strike: "There is only one kind of men who have never been on strike in human history. Every other kind and class have stopped, when they so wished, and have presented demands to the world, claiming to be indispensable—except the men who have carried the world on their shoulders, have kept it alive, have endured torture as sole payment, but have never walked out on the human race. Well, their turn has come. Let the world discover who they are, what they do and what happens when they refuse to function. This is the strike of the men of the mind."

THE MEANING OF MONEY

This is a speech made by Francisco d'Anconia, copper industrialist, heir to an enormous fortune, Galt's closest friend and first to join him in going on strike.

"So you think that money is the root of all evil?" said Francisco d'Anconia. "Have you ever asked what is the root of money? Money is a tool of exchange, which can't exist unless there are goods produced and men able to produce them. Money is the material shape of the principle that men who wish to deal with one another must deal by trade and give value for value. Money is not the tool of the moochers, who claim your product by tears, or of the looters, who take it from you by force. Money is made possible only by the men who produce. Is this what you consider evil?

"When you accept money in payment for your effort, you do so only on the conviction that you will exchange it for the product of the effort of others. It is not the moochers or the looters who give value to money. Not an ocean of tears nor all the guns in the world can transform those pieces of paper in your wallet into the bread you will need to survive tomorrow. Those pieces of paper, which should have been gold, are a token of honor—your claim upon the energy of the men who produce. Your wallet is your statement of hope that somewhere in the world around you there are men who will not default on that moral principle which is the root of money. Is this what you consider evil?

"Have you ever looked for the root of production? Take a look at an electric generator and dare tell yourself that it was created by the muscular effort of unthinking brutes. Try to grow a seed of wheat without the knowledge left to you by men who had to discover it for the first time. Try to obtain your food by means of nothing but physical motions—and you'll learn that man's mind is the root of all the goods produced and of all the wealth that has ever existed on earth.

"But you say that money is made by the strong at the expense of the weak? What strength do you mean? It is not the strength of guns or muscles. Wealth is the product of man's capacity to think. Then is money made by the man who invents a motor at the expense of those who did not invent it? Is money made by the intelligent at the expense of the fools? By the able at the expense of the incompetent? By the ambitious at the expense of the lazy? Money is *made*—before it can be looted or mooched—made by the effort of every honest man, each to the extent of his ability. An honest man is one who knows that he can't consume more than he has produced.

"To trade by means of money is the code of the men of good will. Money rests on the axiom that every man is the owner of his mind and his effort. Money allows no power to prescribe the value of your effort except the voluntary choice of the man who is willing to trade you his effort in return.

Money permits you to obtain for your goods and your labor that which they are worth to the men who buy them, but no more. Money permits no deals except those to mutual benefit by the unforced judgment of the traders. Money demands of you the recognition that men must work for their own benefit, not for their own injury, for their gain, not their loss—the recognition that they are not beasts of burden, born to carry the weight of your misery—that you must offer them values, not wounds—that the common bond among men is not the exchange of suffering, but the exchange of *goods*. Money demands that you sell, not your weakness to men's stupidity, but your talent to their reason; it demands that you buy, not the shoddiest they offer, but the best that your money can find. And when men live by trade—with reason, not force, as their final arbiter—it is the best product that wins, the best performance, the man of best judgment and highest ability—and the degree of a man's productiveness is the degree of his reward. This is the code of existence whose tool and symbol is money. Is this what you consider evil?

"But money is only a tool. It will take you wherever you wish, but it will not replace you as the driver. It will give you the means for the satisfaction of your desires, but it will not provide you with desires. Money is the scourge of the men who attempt to reverse the law of causality—the men who seek to replace the mind by seizing the products of the mind.

"Money will not purchase happiness for the man who has no concept of what he wants: money will not give him a code of values, if he's evaded the knowledge of what to value, and it will not provide him with a purpose, if he's evaded the choice of what to seek. Money will not buy intelligence for the fool, or admiration for the coward, or respect for the incompetent. The man who attempts to purchase the brains of his superiors to serve him, with his money replacing his judgment, ends up by becoming the victim of his inferiors. The men of intelligence desert him, but the cheats and the frauds come flocking to him, drawn by a law which he has not discovered: that no man may be smaller than his money. Is this the reason why you call it evil?

"Only the man who does not need it, is fit to inherit wealth—the man who would make his own fortune no matter where he started. If an heir is equal to his money, it serves him; if not, it destroys him. But you look on and you cry that money corrupted him. Did it? Or did he corrupt his money?

Do not envy a worthless heir; his wealth is not yours and you would have done no better with it. Do not think that it should have been distributed among you; loading the world with fifty parasites instead of one, would not bring back the dead virtue which was the fortune. Money is a living power that dies without its root. Money will not serve the mind that cannot match it. Is this the reason why you call it evil?

"Money is your means of survival. The verdict you pronounce upon the source of your livelihood is the verdict you pronounce upon your life. If the source is corrupt, you have damned your own existence. Did you get your money by fraud? By pandering to men's vices or men's stupidity? By catering to fools, in the hope of getting more than your ability deserves? By lowering your standards? By doing work you despise for purchasers you scorn? If so, then your money will not give you a moment's or a penny's worth of joy. Then all the things you buy will become, not a tribute to you, but a reproach; not an achievement, but a reminder of shame. Then you'll scream that money is evil. Evil, because it would not pinch-hit for your self-respect? Evil, because it would not let you enjoy your depravity? Is this the root of your hatred of money?

"Money will always remain an effect and refuse to replace you as the cause. Money is the product of virtue, but it will not give you virtue and it will not redeem your vices. Money will not give you the unearned, neither in matter nor in spirit. Is this the root of your hatred of money?

"Or did you say it's the *love* of money that's the root of all evil? To love a thing is to know and love its nature. To love money is to know and love the fact that money is the creation of the best power within you, and your passkey to trade your effort for the effort of the best among men. It's the person who would sell his soul for a nickel, who is loudest in proclaiming his hatred of money—and he has good reason to hate it. The lovers of money are willing to work for it. They know they are able to deserve it.

"Let me give you a tip on a clue to men's characters: the man who damns money has obtained it dishonorably; the man who respects it has earned it.

"Run for your life from any man who tells you that money is evil. That sentence is the leper's bell of an approaching looter. So long as men live together on earth and need means to deal with one another—their only substitute, if they abandon money, is the muzzle of a gun.

"But money demands of you the highest virtues, if you wish to make it or to keep it. Men who have no courage, pride or self-esteem, men who have no moral sense of their right to their money and are not willing to defend it as they defend their life, men who apologize for being rich—will not remain rich for long. They are the natural bait for the swarms of looters that stay under rocks for centuries, but come crawling out at the first smell of a man who begs to be forgiven for the guilt of owning wealth. They will hasten to relieve him of the guilt—and of his life, as he deserves.

"Then you will see the rise of the men of the double standard—the men who live by force, yet count on those who live by trade to create the value of their looted money—the men who are the hitchhikers of virtue. In a moral society, these are the criminals, and the statutes are written to protect you against them. But when a society establishes criminals-by-right and looters-by-law—men who use force to seize the wealth of *disarmed* victims—then money becomes its creators' avenger. Such looters believe it safe to rob defenseless men, once they've passed a law to disarm them. But their loot becomes the magnet for other looters, who get it from them as they got it. Then the race goes, not to the ablest at production, but to those most ruthless at brutality. When force is the standard, the murderer wins over the pickpocket. And then that society vanishes, in a spread of ruins and slaughter.

"Do you wish to know whether that day is coming? Watch money. Money is the barometer of a society's virtue. When you see that trading is done, not by consent, but by compulsion—when you see that in order to produce, you need to obtain permission from men who produce nothing—when you see that money is flowing to those who deal, not in goods, but in favors—when you see that men get richer by graft and by pull than by work, and your laws don't protect you against them, but protect them against you—when you see corruption being rewarded and honesty becoming a self-sacrifice—you may know that your society is doomed. Money is so noble a medium that it does not compete with guns and it does not make terms with brutality. It will not permit a country to survive as half-property, half-loot.

"Whenever destroyers appear among men, they start by destroying money, for money is men's protection and the base of a moral existence. Destroyers seize gold and leave to its owners a counterfeit pile of paper. This kills all objective standards and delivers men into the arbitrary power of an arbitrary setter of values. Gold was an objective value, an equivalent of wealth produced. Paper is a mortgage on wealth that does not exist, backed by a gun aimed at those who are expected to produce it. Paper is a check drawn by legal looters upon an account which is not theirs: upon the virtue of the victims. Watch for the day when it bounces, marked: 'Account overdrawn.'

"When you have made evil the means of survival, do not expect men to remain good. Do not expect them to stay moral and lose their lives for the purpose of becoming the fodder of the immoral. Do not expect them to produce, when production is punished and looting rewarded. Do not ask, 'Who is destroying the world?' You are.

"You stand in the midst of the greatest achievements of the greatest productive civilization and you wonder why it's crumbling around you, while you're damning its life-blood—money. You look upon money as the savages did before you, and you wonder why the jungle is creeping back to the edge of your cities. Throughout men's history, money was always seized by looters of one brand or another, whose names changed, but whose method remained the same: to seize wealth by force and to keep the producers bound, demeaned, defamed, deprived of honor. That phrase about the evil of money, which you mouth with such righteous recklessness, comes from a time when wealth was produced by the labor of slaves—slaves who repeated the motions once discovered by somebody's mind and left unimproved for centuries. So long as production was ruled by force, and wealth was obtained by conquest, there was little to conquer. Yet through all the centuries of stagnation and starvation, men exalted the looters, as aristocrats of the sword, as aristocrats of birth, as aristocrats of the bureau, and despised the producers, as slaves, as traders, as shopkeepers—as industrialists.

"To the glory of mankind, there was, for the first and only time in history, a *country of money*—and I have no higher, more reverent tribute to pay to America, for this means: a country of reason, justice, freedom, production, achievement.

For the first time, man's mind and money were set free, and there were no fortunes-by-conquest, but only fortunes-by-work, and instead of swordsmen and slaves, there appeared the real maker of wealth, the greatest worker, the highest type of human being—the self-made man—the American industrialist.

"If you ask me to name the proudest distinction of Americans, I would choose—because it contains all the others—the fact that they were the people who created the phrase 'to *make* money.' No other language or nation had ever used these words before; men had always thought of wealth as a static quantity—to be seized, begged, inherited, shared, looted or obtained as a favor. Americans were the first to understand that wealth has to be created. The words 'to make money' hold the essence of human morality.

"Yet these were the words for which Americans were denounced by the rotted cultures of the looters' continents. Now the looters' credo has brought you to regard your proudest achievements as a hallmark of shame, your prosperity as guilt, your greatest men, the industrialists, as blackguards, and your magnificent factories as the product and property of muscular labor, the labor of whip-driven slaves, like the pyramids of Egypt. The rotter who simpers that he sees no difference between the power of the dollar and the power of the whip, ought to learn the difference on his own hide—as, I think, he will.

"Until and unless you discover that money is the root of all good, you ask for your own destruction. When money ceases to be the tool by which men deal with one another, then men become the tools of men. Blood, whips and guns —or dollars. Take your choice—there is no other—and your time is running out."

THE MARTYRDOM OF THE INDUSTRIALISTS

This is part of a conversation between Francisco d'Anconia and Hank Rearden, a self-made man who has risen to the position of the country's greatest steel industrialist. (Francisco speaking.)

"You, who would not submit to the hardships of nature, but set out to conquer it and placed it in the service of your joy and your comfort—to what have you submitted at the hands of men? You, who know from your work that one bears punishment only for being wrong—what have you been willing to bear and for what reason? All your life, you have heard yourself denounced, not for your faults, but for your greatest virtues. You have been hated, not for your mistakes, but for your achievements. You have been scorned for all those qualities of character which are your highest pride. You have been called selfish for the courage of acting on your own judgment and bearing sole responsibility for your own life. You have been called arrogant for your independent mind. You have been called cruel for your unyielding integrity. You have been called anti-social for the vision that made you venture upon undiscovered roads. You have been called ruthless for the strength and self-discipline of your drive to your purpose. You have been called greedy for the magnificence of your power to create wealth. You, who've expended an inconceivable flow of energy, have been called a parasite. You, who've created abundance where there had been nothing but wastelands and helpless, starving men before you, have been called a robber. You, who've kept them all alive, have been called an exploiter. You, the purest and most moral man among them, have been sneered at as a 'vulgar materialist.' Have you stopped to ask them: by what right?—by what code?—by what standard? No, you have borne it all and kept silent. You bowed to their code and you never upheld your own. You knew what exacting morality was needed to produce a single metal nail, but you let them brand you as immoral. You knew that man needs the strictest code of values to deal with nature, but you thought that you needed no such code to deal with men. You left the deadliest weapon in the hands of your enemies, a weapon you never suspected or understood. Their moral code is their weapon. Ask yourself how deeply and in how many terrible ways you have accepted it. Ask yourself what it is that a code of moral values does to a man's life, and why he can't exist without it, and what happens to him if he accepts the wrong standard, by which the evil is the good. Shall I tell you why you're drawn to me, even though you think you ought to damn me? It's because I'm the first man who has given you what the whole world owes you and what you should have demanded of all men before you dealt with them: a moral sanction....

"You're guilty of a great sin, Mr. Rearden, much guiltier than they tell you, but not in the way they preach. The worst guilt is to accept an undeserved guilt—and that is what you have been doing all your life. You have been paying blackmail, not for your vices, but for your virtues. You have been willing to carry the load of an unearned punishment—and to let it grow the heavier the greater the virtues you practiced. But your virtues were those which keep men alive. Your own moral code—the one you lived by, but never stated, acknowledged or defended—was the code that preserves man's existence. If you were punished for it, what was the nature of those who punished you? Yours was the code of life. What, then, is theirs? What standard of value lies at its root? What is its ultimate purpose? Do you think that what you're facing is merely a conspiracy to seize your wealth? You, who know the source of wealth, should know it's much more and much worse than that. Did you ask me to name man's motive power? Man's motive power is his moral code. Ask yourself where their code is leading you and what it offers you as your final goal. A viler evil than to murder a man, is to sell him suicide as an act of virtue. A viler evil than to throw a man into a sacrificial furnace, is to demand that he leap in, of his own will, and that he build the furnace, besides. By their own statement, it is *they* who need you and have nothing to offer you in return. By their own statement, you must support them because they cannot survive without you. Consider the obscenity of offering their impotence and their need—their need of *you*—as a justification for your torture. Are you willing to accept it? Do you care to purchase—at the price of your great endurance, at the price of your agony—the satisfaction of the needs of your own destroyers?...

"If you saw Atlas, the giant who holds the world on his shoulders, if you saw that he stood, blood running down his chest, his knees buckling, his arms trembling but still trying to hold the world aloft with the last of his strength, and the greater his effort the heavier the world bore down upon his shoulders—what would you tell him to do?"

"I . . . don't know. What . . . could he do? What would *you* tell him?"

"To shrug."

THE MORAL MEANING OF CAPITALISM

This is a statement made by Hank Rearden at his trial for an illegal sale of a metal alloy which he had created and which has been placed under government rationing and control.

"I do not want my attitude to be misunderstood. I shall be glad to state it for the record. . . . I work for nothing but my own profit—which I make by selling a product they need to men who are willing and able to buy it. I do not produce it for their benefit at the expense of mine, and they do not buy it for my benefit at the expense of theirs; I do not sacrifice my interests to them nor do they sacrifice theirs to me; we deal as equals by mutual consent to mutual advantage —and I am proud of every penny that I have earned in this manner. I am rich and I am proud of every penny I own. I have made my money by my own effort, in free exchange and through the voluntary consent of every man I dealt with —the voluntary consent of those who employed me when I started, the voluntary consent of those who work for me now, the voluntary consent of those who buy my product. I shall answer all the questions you are afraid to ask me openly. Do I wish to pay my workers more than their services are worth to me? I do not. Do I wish to sell my product for less than my customers are willing to pay me? I do not. Do I wish to sell it at a loss or give it away? I do not. If this is evil, do whatever you please about me, according to whatever standards you hold. These are mine. I am earning my own living, as every honest man must. I refuse to accept as guilt the fact of my own existence and the fact that I must work in order to support it. I refuse to accept as guilt the fact that I am able to do it and to do it well. I refuse to accept as guilt the fact that I am able to do it better than most people— the fact that my work is of greater value than the work of my neighbors and that more men are willing to pay me. I refuse to apologize for my ability—I refuse to apologize for my success—I refuse to apologize for my money. If this is evil, make the most of it. If this is what the public finds harmful to its interests let the public destroy me. This is my code—and I will accept no other. I could say to you that I have done more good for my fellow man than you can ever hope to accomplish—but I will not say it, because I do not seek the good of others as a sanction for my right to exist, nor do I recognize the good of others as a justification for their seizure of my property or their destruction of my life. I will not say that the good of others was the purpose of my work—my own good was my purpose, and I despise the man who surrenders his. I could say to you that you do not serve the public good— that nobody's good can be achieved at the price of human sacrifices—that when you violate the rights of one man, you have violated the rights of all, and a public of rightless creatures is doomed to destruction. I could say to you that you will and can achieve nothing but universal devastation—as any looter must, when he runs out of victims. I could say it, but I won't. It is not your particular policy that I challenge, but your moral premise. If it were true that men could achieve their good by means of turning some men into sacrificial animals, and I were asked to immolate myself for the sake of creatures who wanted to survive at the price of my blood, if I were asked to serve the interests of society apart from, above and against my own—I would refuse, I would reject it as the most contemptible evil, I would fight it with every power I possess, I would fight the whole of mankind, if one minute were all I could last before I were murdered, I would fight in the full confidence of the justice of my battle and of a living being's right to exist. Let there be no misunderstanding about me. If it is now the belief of my fellow men, who call themselves the public, that their good requires victims, then I say: The public good be damned, I will have no part of it!"

THE MEANING OF SEX

This is from a conversation between Francisco d'Anconia and Hank Rearden, who are in love with the same woman, though neither one of them knows it. (Francisco speaking.)

"Do you remember what I said about money and about the men who seek to reverse the law of cause and effect? The men who try to replace the mind by seizing the products of the mind? Well, the man who despises himself tries to gain self-esteem from sexual adventures—which can't be done, because sex is not the cause, but an effect and an expression of a man's sense of his own value. . . .

"The men who think that wealth comes from material resources and has no intellectual root or meaning, are the men who think—for the same reason—that sex is a physical capacity which functions independently of one's mind, choice or code of values. They think that your body creates a desire and makes a choice for you—just about in some such way as if iron ore transformed itself into railroad rails of its own volition. Love is blind, they say; sex is impervious to reason and mocks the power of all philosophers. But, in fact, a man's sexual choice is the result and the sum of his fundamental convictions. Tell me what a man finds sexually attractive and I will tell you his entire philosophy of life. Show me the woman he sleeps with and I will tell you his valuation of himself. No matter what corruption he's taught about the virtue of selflessness, sex is the most profoundly selfish of all acts, an act which he cannot perform for any motive but his own enjoyment—just try to think of performing it in a spirit of selfless charity!—an act which is not possible in self-abasement, only in self-exaltation, only in the confidence of being desired and being worthy of desire. It is an act that forces him to stand naked in spirit, as well as in body, and to accept his real ego as his standard of value. He will always be attracted to the woman who reflects his deepest vision of himself, the woman whose surrender permits him to experience —or to fake—a sense of self-esteem. The man who is proudly certain of his own value, will want the highest type of woman he can find, the woman he admires, the strongest, the hardest to conquer—because only the possession of a heroine will give him the sense of an achievement, not the possession of a brainless slut. . . . He does not seek to gain his value, he seeks to express it. There is no conflict between the standards of his mind and the desires of his body.

"But the man who is convinced of his own worthlessness will be drawn to a woman he despises—because she will reflect his own secret self, she will release him from that objective reality in which he is a fraud, she will give him a momentary illusion of his own value and a momentary escape from the moral code that damns him. Observe the ugly mess which most men make of their sex lives—and observe the mess of contradictions which they hold as their moral philosophy. One proceeds from the other. Love is our response to our highest values—and can be nothing else. Let a man corrupt his values and his view of existence, let him profess that love is not self-enjoyment but self-denial, that virtue consists, not of pride, but of pity or pain or weakness or sacrifice, that the noblest love is born, not of admiration, but of charity, not in response to *values*, but in response to *flaws*—and he will have cut himself in two. His body will not obey him, it will not respond, it will make him impotent toward the woman he professes to love and draw him to the lowest type of whore he can find. His body will always follow the ultimate logic of his deepest convictions; if he believes that flaws are values, he has damned existence as evil and only the evil will attract him. He has damned himself and he will feel that depravity is all he is worthy of enjoying. He has equated virtue with pain and he will feel that vice is the only realm of pleasure. Then he will scream that his body has vicious desires of its own which his mind cannot conquer, that sex is sin, that true love is a pure emotion of the spirit. And then he will wonder why love brings him nothing but boredom, and sex—nothing but shame. . . .

"You'd never accept any part of their vicious creed. You wouldn't be able to force it upon yourself. If you tried to damn sex as evil, you'd still find yourself, against your will, acting on the proper moral premise. You'd be attracted to the highest woman you met. You'd always want a heroine. You'd be incapable of self-contempt. You'd be unable to believe that existence is evil and that you're a helpless creature caught in an impossible universe. You're the man who's spent his life shaping matter to the purpose of his mind. You're the man who would know that just as an idea unexpressed in physical action is contemptible hypocrisy, so is platonic love—and just as physical action unguided by an idea is a fool's self-fraud, so is sex when cut off from one's code of values. It's the same issue, and you would know it. Your inviolate sense of self-esteem would know it. You would be incapable of desire for a woman you despised. Only the man who extols the purity of a love devoid of desire, is capable of the depravity of a desire devoid of love. But observe that most people are creatures cut in half who keep swinging desperately to one side or to the other. One kind of half is the man who despises money, factories, skyscrapers and his own body. He holds undefined emotions about non-conceivable subjects as the meaning of life and as his claim to virtue. And he cries with despair, because he can feel nothing for the women he respects, but finds himself in bondage to an irresistible passion for a slut from the gutter. He is the man whom people call an idealist. The other kind of half is the man whom people call practical, the man who despises principles, abstractions, art, philosophy and his own mind. He regards the acquisition of material objects as the only goal of existence—and he laughs at the need to consider their purpose or their source. He expects them to give him pleasure—and he wonders why the more he gets, the less he feels. *He* is the man who spends his time chasing women. Observe the triple fraud which he perpetrates upon himself. He will not acknowledge his need of self-esteem, since he scoffs at such a concept as moral values; yet he feels the profound self-contempt which comes from believing that he is a piece of meat. He will not acknowledge, but he knows that sex is the physical expression of a tribute to personal values. So he tries, by going through the motions of the effect, to acquire that which should have been the cause. He tries to gain a sense of his own value from the women who surrender to him—and he forgets that the women he picks have neither character nor judgment nor standard of value. He tells himself that all he's after is physical pleasure—but observe that he tires of his women in a week or a night, that he despises professional whores and that he loves to imagine he is seducing virtuous girls who make a great exception for his sake. It is the feeling of achievement that he seeks and never finds. What glory can there be in the conquest of a mindless body?"

"FROM EACH ACCORDING TO HIS ABILITY, TO EACH ACCORDING TO HIS NEED"

This is the story of what happened at the Twentieth Century Motor Company, which put the above slogan into practice —as told by one of the survivors.

"Well there was something that happened at that plant where I worked for twenty years. It was when the old man died and his heirs took over. There were three of them, two sons and a daughter, and they brought a new plan to run the factory. They let us vote on it, too, and everybody—almost everybody—voted for it. We didn't know. We thought it was good. No, that's not true, either. We thought that we were supposed to think it was good. The plan was that everybody in the factory would work according to his ability, but would be paid according to his need. . . .

"We voted for that plan at a big meeting, with all of us present, six thousand of us, everybody that worked in the factory. The Starnes heirs made long speeches about it, and it wasn't too clear, but nobody asked any questions. None of us knew just how the plan would work, but every one of us thought that the next fellow knew it. And if anybody had doubts, he felt guilty and kept his mouth shut—because they made it sound like anyone who'd oppose the plan was a child-killer at heart and less than a human being. They told us that this plan would achieve a noble ideal. Well, how were we to know otherwise? Hadn't we heard it all our lives—from our parents and our schoolteachers and our ministers, and in every newspaper we ever read and every movie and every public speech? Hadn't we always been told that this was righteous and just? Well, maybe there's some excuse for what we did at that meeting. Still, we voted for the plan—and what we got, we had it coming to us. You know, ma'am, we are marked men, in a way, those of us who lived through the four years of that plan in the Twentieth Century factory. What is it that hell is supposed to be? Evil—plain, naked, smirking evil, isn't it? Well, that's what we saw and helped to make—and I think we're damned, every one of us, and maybe we'll never be forgiven. . . .

"Do you know how it worked, that plan, and what it did to people? Try pouring water into a tank where there's a pipe at the bottom draining it out faster than you pour it, and each bucket you bring breaks that pipe an inch wider, and the harder you work the more is demanded of you, and you stand slinging buckets forty hours a week, then forty-eight, then fifty-six—for your neighbor's supper—for his wife's operation—for his child's measles—for his mother's wheel chair—for his uncle's shirt—for his nephew's schooling—for the baby next door—for the baby to be born—

for anyone anywhere around you—it's theirs to receive, from diapers to dentures—and yours to work, from sunup to sundown, month after month, year after year, with nothing to show for it but your sweat, with nothing in sight for you but their pleasure, for the whole of your life, without rest, without hope, without end. . . . From each according to his ability, to each according to his need. . . .

"We're all one big family, they told us, we're all in this together. But you don't all stand working an acetylene torch ten hours a day—together, and you don't all get a belly-ache—together. What's whose ability and which of whose needs comes first? When it's all one pot, you can't let any man decide what his own needs are, can you? If you did, he might claim that he needs a yacht—and if his feelings is all you have to go by, he might prove it, too. Why not? If it's not right for me to own a car until I've worked myself into a hospital ward, earning a car for every loafer and every naked savage on earth—why can't he demand a yacht from me, too, if I still have the ability not to have collapsed? No? He can't? Then why can he demand that I go without cream for my coffee until he's replastered his living room? . . . Oh well . . . Well, anyway, it was decided that nobody had the right to judge his own need or ability. We *voted* on it. Yes, ma'am, we voted on it in a public meeting twice a year. How else could it be done? Do you care to think what would happen at such a meeting? It took us just one meeting to discover that we had become beggars—rotten, whining, sniveling beggars, all of us, because no man could claim his pay as his rightful earning, he had no rights and no earnings, his work didn't belong to him, it belonged to 'the family,' and they owed him nothing in return, and the only claim he had on them was his 'need'—so he had to beg in public for relief from his needs, like any lousy moocher, listing all his troubles and miseries, down to his patched drawers and his wife's head colds, hoping that 'the family' would throw him the alms. He had to claim miseries, because it's miseries, not work, that had become the coin of the realm—so it turned into a contest among six thousand panhandlers, each claiming that *his* need was worse than his brother's. How else could it be done? Do you care to guess what happened, what sort of men kept quiet, feeling shame, and what sort got away with the jackpot?

"But that wasn't all. There was something else that we discovered at the same meeting. The factory's production had fallen by forty per cent, in that first half-year, so it was decided that somebody hadn't delivered 'according to his ability.' Who? How would you tell it? 'The family' voted on that, too. They voted which men were the best, and these men were sentenced to work overtime each night for the next six months. Overtime without pay—because you weren't paid by time and you weren't paid by work, only by need.

"Do I have to tell you what happened after that—and into what sort of creatures we all started turning, we who had once been human? We began to hide whatever ability we had, to slow down and watch like hawks that we never worked any faster or better than the next fellow. What else could we do, when we knew that if we did our best for 'the family,' it's not thanks or rewards that we'd get, but punishment? We knew that for every stinker who'd ruin a batch of motors and cost the company money—either through his sloppiness, because he didn't have to care, or through plain incompetence—it's we who'd have to pay with our nights and our Sundays. So we did our best to be no good.

"There was one young boy who started out, full of fire for the noble ideal, a bright kid without any schooling, but with a wonderful head on his shoulders. The first year, he figured out a work process that saved us thousands of man-hours. He gave it to 'the family,' didn't ask anything for it, either, couldn't ask, but that was all right with him. It was for the ideal, he said. But when he found himself voted as one of our ablest and sentenced to night work, because we hadn't gotten enough from him, he shut his mouth and his brain. You can bet he didn't come up with any ideas, the second year.

"What was it they'd always told us about the vicious competition of the profit system, where men had to compete for who'd do a better job than his fellows? Vicious, wasn't it? Well, they should have seen what it was like when we all had to compete with one another for who'd do the worst job possible. There's no surer way to destroy a man than to force him into a spot where he has to aim at *not* doing his best, where he has to struggle to do a bad job, day after day. That will finish him quicker than drink or idleness or pulling stick-ups for a living. But there was nothing else for us to do except to fake unfitness. The one accusation we feared was to be suspected of ability. Ability was like a mortgage on you that you could never pay off. And what was there to work for? You knew that your basic pittance would be given to you anyway, whether you worked or not—your 'housing and feeding allowance,' it was called—and above that pittance, you had no chance to get anything, no matter how hard you tried. You couldn't count on buying a new suit of clothes next year—they might give you a 'clothing allowance' or they might not, according to whether nobody broke a leg, needed an operation or gave birth to more babies. And if there wasn't enough money for new suits for everybody, then you couldn't get yours, either.

"There was one man who'd worked hard all his life, because he'd always wanted to send his son through college. Well, the boy graduated from high school in the second year of the plan—but 'the family' wouldn't give the father any 'allowance' for the college. They said his son couldn't go to college, until we had enough to send everybody's sons to college—and that we first had to send everybody's children through high school, and we didn't even have enough for that. The father died the following year, in a knife fight with somebody in a saloon, a fight over nothing in particular—such fights were beginning to happen among us all the time.

"Then there was an old guy, a widower with no family, who had one hobby: phonograph records. I guess that was all he ever got out of life. In the old days, he used to skip meals just to buy himself some new recording of classical music. Well, they didn't give him any 'allowance' for records—'personal luxury,' they called it. But at that same meeting, Millie Bush, somebody's daughter, a mean, ugly little eight-year-old, was voted a pair of gold braces for her buck teeth—this was 'medical need,' because the staff psychologist had said that the poor girl would get an inferiority complex if her teeth weren't straightened out. The old guy who loved music, turned to drink, instead. He got so you never saw him fully conscious any more. But it seems like there was one thing he couldn't forget. One night, he came staggering down the street, saw Millie Bush, swung his fist and knocked all her teeth out. Every one of them.

"Drink, of course, was what we all turned to, some more, some less. Don't ask how we got the money for it. When all the decent pleasures are forbidden, there's always ways to get the rotten ones. You don't break into grocery stores after dark and you don't pick your fellow's pockets to buy classical symphonies or fishing tackle, but if it's to get stinking drunk and forget—you do. Fishing tackle? Hunting guns? Snapshot cameras? Hobbies? There wasn't any 'amusement allowance' for anybody. 'Amusement' was the first thing they dropped. Aren't you always supposed to be ashamed to object when anybody asks you to give up anything, if it's something that gave you pleasure? Even our 'tobacco allowance' was cut to where we got two packs of cigarettes a month—and this, they told us, was because the money had to go into the babies' milk fund. Babies was the only item of production that didn't fall, but rose and kept on rising—because people had nothing else to do, I guess, and because they didn't have to care, the baby wasn't their burden, it was 'the family's.' In fact, the best chance you had of getting a raise and breathing easier for a while was a 'baby allowance.' Either that, or a major disease.

"It didn't take us long to see how it all worked out. Any man who tried to play straight, had to refuse himself everything. He lost his taste for any pleasure, he hated to smoke a nickel's worth of tobacco or chew a stick of gum, worrying whether somebody had more need for that nickel. He felt ashamed of every mouthful of food he swallowed, wondering whose weary nights of overtime had paid for it, knowing that his food was not his by right, miserably wishing to be cheated rather than to cheat, to be a sucker, but not a blood-sucker. He wouldn't marry, he wouldn't help his folks back home, he wouldn't put an extra burden on 'the family.' Besides, if he still had some sort of sense of responsibility, he couldn't marry or bring children into the world, when he could plan nothing, promise nothing, count on nothing. But the shiftless and the irresponsible had a field day of it. They bred babies, they got girls into trouble, they dragged in every worthless relative they had from all over the country, every unmarried pregnant sister, for an extra 'disability allowance,' they got more sicknesses than any doctor could disprove, they ruined their clothing, their furniture, their homes—what the hell, 'the family' was paying for it! They found more ways of getting in 'need' than the rest of us could ever imagine—they developed a special skill for it, which was the only ability *they* showed.

"God help us, ma'am! Do you see what we saw? We saw that we'd been given a law to live by, a *moral* law, they called it, which punished those who observed it—for observing it. The more you tried to live up to it, the more you suffered; the more you cheated it, the bigger reward you got. Your honesty was like a tool left at the mercy of the next man's dishonesty. The honest ones paid, the dishonest collected. The honest lost, the dishonest won. How long could men stay good under this sort of law of goodness? We were a pretty decent bunch of fellows when we started. There weren't many chiselers among us. We knew our jobs and we were proud of it and we worked for the best factory in the country, where old man Starnes hired nothing but the pick of the country's labor. Within one year under the new plan, there wasn't an honest man left among us. *That* was the evil, the sort of hell-horror evil that preachers used to scare you with, but you never thought to see alive. Not that the plan encouraged a few bastards, but that it turned decent people into bastards, and there was nothing else that it could do—and it was called a moral ideal!

"What was it we were supposed to want to work for? For the love of our brothers? What brothers? For the bums, the loafers, the moochers we saw all around us? And whether they were cheating or plain incompetent, whether they were unwilling or unable—what difference did that make to us? If we were tied for life to the level of their unfitness, faked or real, how long could we care to go on? We had no way of knowing their ability, we had no way of controlling their needs—all we knew was that we were beasts of burden struggling blindly in some sort of place that was half-hospital, half-stockyards—a place geared to nothing but disability, disaster, disease—beasts put there for the relief of whatever whoever chose to say was whichever's need.

"Love of our brothers? That's when we learned to hate our brothers for the first time in our lives. We began to hate them for every meal they swallowed, for every small pleasure they enjoyed, for one man's new shirt, for another's wife's hat, for an outing with their family, for a paint job on their house —it was taken from us, it was paid for by our privations, our denials, our hunger. We began to spy on one another, each hoping to catch the others lying about their needs, so as to cut their 'allowance' at the next meeting. We began to have stool pigeons who informed on people, who reported that somebody had bootlegged a turkey to his family on some Sunday —which he'd paid for by gambling, most likely. We began to meddle into one another's lives. We provoked family quarrels, to get somebody's relatives thrown out. Any time we saw a man starting to go steady with a girl, we made life miserable for him. We broke up many engagements. We didn't want anyone to marry, we didn't want any more dependents to feed.

"In the old days, we used to celebrate if somebody had a baby, we used to chip in and help him out with the hospital bills, if he happened to be hard-pressed for the moment. Now, if a baby was born, we didn't speak to the parents for weeks. Babies, to us, had become what locusts were to farmers. In the old days, we used to help a man if he had a bad illness in the family. Now—well, I'll tell you about just one case. It was the mother of a man who had been with us for fifteen years. She was a kindly old lady, cheerful and wise, she knew us all by our first names and we all liked her—we used to like her. One day, she slipped on the cellar stairs and fell and broke her hip. We knew what that meant at her age. The staff doctor said that she'd have to be sent to a hospital in town, for expensive treatments that would take a long time. The old lady died the night before she was to leave for town. They never established the cause of death. No, I don't know whether she was murdered. Nobody said that. Nobody would talk about it at all. All I know is that I—and that's what I can't forget!—I, too, had caught myself wishing that she would die. This—may God forgive us!—was the brotherhood, the security, the abundance that the plan was supposed to achieve for us!

"Was there any reason why this sort of horror would ever be preached by anybody? Was there anybody who got any profit from it? There was. The Starnes heirs. I hope you're not going to remind me that they'd sacrificed a fortune and turned the factory over to us as a gift. We were fooled by that one, too. Yes, they gave up the factory. But profit, ma'am, depends on what it is you're after. And what the Starnes heirs were after, no money on earth could buy. Money is too clean and innocent for that.

"Eric Starnes, the youngest—he was a jellyfish that didn't have the guts to be after anything in particular. He got himself voted as Director of our Public Relations Department, which didn't do anything, except that he had a staff for the not doing of anything, so he didn't have to bother sticking around the office. The pay he got—well, I shouldn't call it 'pay,' none of us was 'paid'—the alms voted to him was fairly modest, about ten times what I got, but that wasn't riches. Eric didn't care for money—he wouldn't have known what to do with it. He spent his time hanging around among us, showing how chummy he was and democratic. He wanted to be loved, it seems. The way he went about it was to keep reminding us that he had given us the factory. We couldn't stand him.

"Gerald Starnes was our Director of Production. We never learned just what the size of his rake-off—his alms—had been. It would have taken a staff of accountants to figure that out, and a staff of engineers to trace the way it was piped, directly or indirectly, into his office. None of it was supposed to be for him—it was all for company expenses. Gerald had three cars, four secretaries, five telephones, and he used to throw champagne and caviar parties that no tax-paying tycoon in the country could have afforded. He spent more money in one year than his father had earned in profits in the last two years of his life. We saw a hundred-pound stack—a hundred pounds, we weighed them—of magazines in Gerald's office, full of stories about our factory and our noble plan, with big pictures of Gerald Starnes, calling him a great social crusader. Gerald liked to come into the shops at night, dressed in his formal clothes, flashing diamond cuff links the size of a nickel and shaking cigar ashes all over. Any cheap show-off who's got nothing to parade but his cash, is bad enough—except that he makes no bones about the cash being his, and you're free to gape at him or not, as you wish, and mostly you don't. But when a bastard like Gerald Starnes puts on an act and keeps spouting that he doesn't care for material wealth, that he's only serving 'the family,' that all the lushness is not for himself, but for our sake and for the common good, because it's necessary to keep up the prestige of the company and of the noble plan in the eyes of the public—then that's when you learn to hate the creature as you've never hated anything human.

"But his sister Ivy was worse. She really did not care for material wealth. The alms she got was no bigger than ours, and she went about in scuffed, flat-heeled shoes and shirt-waists—just to show how selfless she was. She was our Director of Distribution. She was the lady in charge of our needs. She was the one who held us by the throat. Of course, distribution was supposed to be decided by voting—by the voice of the people. But when the people are six thousand howling voices, trying to decide without yardstick, rhyme or reason, when there are no rules to the game and each can demand anything, but has a right to nothing, when everybody holds power over everybody's life except his own—then it turns out, as it did, that the voice of the people is Ivy Starnes. By the end of the second year, we dropped the pretense of the 'family meetings'—in the name of 'production efficiency and time economy,' one meeting used to take ten days—and all the petitions of need were simply sent to Miss Starnes' office. No, not sent. They had to be recited to her in person by every petitioner. Then she made up a distribution list, which she read to us for our vote of approval at a meeting that lasted three-quarters of an hour. We voted approval. There was a ten-minute period on the agenda for discussion and objections. We made no objections. We knew better by that time. Nobody can divide a factory's income among thousands of people, without some sort of a gauge to measure people's value. Her gauge was bootlicking. Selfless? In her father's time, all of his money wouldn't have given him a chance to speak to his lousiest wiper and get away with it, as she spoke to our best skilled workers and their wives. She had pale eyes that looked fishy, cold and dead. And if you ever want to see pure evil, you should have seen the way her eyes glinted when she watched some man who'd talked back to her once and who'd just heard his name on the list of those getting nothing above basic pittance. And when you saw it, you saw the real motive of any person who's ever preached the slogan: 'From each according to his ability, to each according to his need.'

"This was the whole secret of it. At first, I kept wondering how it could be possible that the educated, the cultured, the famous men of the world could make a mistake of this size and preach, as righteousness, this sort of abomination—when five minutes of thought should have told them what would happen if somebody tried to practice what they preached. Now I know that they didn't do it by any kind of mistake. Mistakes of this size are never made innocently. If men fall for some vicious piece of insanity, when they have no way to make it work and no possible reason to explain their choice—it's because they have a reason that they do not wish to tell. And we weren't so innocent either, when we voted for that plan at the first meeting. We didn't do it just because we believed that the drippy old guff they spewed was good. We had another reason, but the guff helped us to hide it from our neighbors and from ourselves. The guff gave us a chance to pass off as virtue something that we'd be ashamed to admit otherwise. There wasn't a man voting for it who didn't think that under a setup of this kind he'd muscle in on the profits of the men abler than himself. There wasn't a man rich and smart enough but that he didn't think that somebody was richer and smarter, and this plan would give him a share of his better's wealth and brain. But while he was thinking that he'd get unearned benefits from the men above, he forgot about the men below who'd get unearned benefits, too. He forgot about all his inferiors who'd rush to drain him just as he hoped to drain his superiors. The worker who liked the idea that his need entitled him to a limousine like his boss's, forgot that every bum and beggar on earth would come howling that *their* need entitled them to an icebox like his own. *That* was our real motive when we voted—that was the truth of it—but we didn't like to think it, so the less we liked it, the louder we yelled about our love for the common good.

"Well, we got what we asked for. By the time we saw what it was that we'd asked for, it was too late. We were trapped, with no place to go. The best men among us left the factory in the first week of the plan. We lost our best engineers, superintendents, foremen and highest-skilled workers. A man of self-respect doesn't turn into a milch cow for anybody. Some able fellows tried to stick it out, but they couldn't take it for long. We kept losing our men, they kept escaping from the factory like from a pesthole—till we had nothing left except the men of need, but none of the men of ability.

"And the few of us who were still any good, but stayed on, were only those who had been there too long. In the old days, nobody ever quit the Twentieth Century—and, somehow, we couldn't make ourselves believe that it was gone. After a while, we couldn't quit, because no other employer would have us—for which I can't blame him. Nobody would deal with us in any way, no respectable person or firm. All the small shops, where we traded, started moving out of Starnesville fast—till we had nothing left but saloons, gambling joints and crooks who sold us trash at gouging prices. The alms we got kept falling, but the cost of our living went up. The list of the factory's needy kept stretching, but the list of its customers shrank. There was less and less income to divide among more and more people. In the old days, it used to be said that the Twentieth Century Motor trademark was as good as the karat mark on gold. I don't know what it was that the Starnes heirs thought, if they thought at all, but I suppose that like all social planners and like savages, they thought that this trademark was a magic stamp which did the trick by some sort of voodoo power and that it would keep them rich, as it had kept their father. Well, when our customers began to see that we never delivered an order on time and never put out a motor that didn't have something wrong with it—the magic stamp began to work the other way around: people wouldn't take a motor as a gift, if it was marked Twentieth Century. And it came to where our only customers were men who never paid and never meant to pay their bills. But Gerald Starnes, doped by his own publicity, got huffy and went around, with an air of moral superiority, demanding that businessmen place orders with us, not because our motors were good, but because we *needed* the orders so badly.

"By that time, a village half-wit could see what generations of professors had pretended not to notice. What good would our need do to a power plant when its generators stopped because of our defective engines? What good would it do to a man caught on an operating table when the electric light went out? What good would it do to the passengers of a plane when its motor failed in mid-air? And if they bought our product, not because of its merit, but because of our need, would that be the good, the right, the moral thing to do for the owner of that power plant, the surgeon in that hospital, the maker of that plane?

"Yet this was the moral law that the professors and leaders and thinkers had wanted to establish all over the earth. If this is what it did in a single small town where we all knew one another, do you care to think what it would do on a world scale? Do you care to imagine what it would be like, if you had to live and to work, when you're tied to all the disasters and all the malingering of the globe? To work—and whenever any men failed anywhere, it's you who would have to make up for it. To work—with no chance to rise, with your meals and your clothes and your home and your pleasure depending on any swindle, any famine, any pestilence anywhere on earth. To work—with no chance for an extra ration, till the Cambodians have been fed and the Patagonians have been sent through college. To work—on a blank check held by every creature born, by men whom you'll never see, whose needs you'll never know, whose ability or laziness or sloppiness or fraud you have no way to learn and no right to question—just to work and work and work—and leave it up to the Ivys and the Geralds of the world to decide whose stomach will consume the effort, the dreams and the days of your life. And *this* is the moral law to accept? *This*—a moral ideal?

Well, we tried it—and we learned. Our agony took four years, from our first meeting to our last, and it ended the only way it could end: in bankruptcy. At our last meeting, Ivy Starnes was the one who tried to brazen it out. She made a short, nasty, snippy little speech in which she said that the plan had failed because the rest of the country had not accepted it, that a single community could not succeed in the midst of a selfish, greedy world—and that the plan was a noble ideal, but human nature was not good enough for it. A young boy—the one who had been punished for giving us a useful idea in our first year—got up, as we all sat silent, and walked straight to Ivy Starnes on the platform. He said nothing. He spat in her face. That was the end of the noble plan and of the Twentieth Century."

THE FORGOTTEN MAN OF SOCIALIZED MEDICINE

This is the explanation given by a distinguished brain surgeon of why he joined Galt's strike.

"I quit when medicine was placed under State control, some years ago," said Dr. Hendricks. "Do you know what it takes to perform a brain operation? Do you know the kind of skill it demands, and the years of passionate, merciless, excruciating devotion that go to acquire that skill? *That* was what I would not place at the disposal of men whose sole qualification to rule me was their capacity to spout the fraudulent generalities that got them elected to the privilege of enforcing their wishes at the point of a gun. I would not let them dictate the purpose for which my years of study had been spent, or the conditions of my work, or my choice of patients, or the amount of my reward. I observed that in all the discussions that preceded the enslavement of medicine, men discussed everything—except the desires of the doctors. Men considered only the 'welfare' of the patients, with no thought for those who were to provide it. That a doctor should have any right, desire or choice in the matter, was regarded as irrelevant selfishness; his is not to choose, they said, only 'to serve.' That a man who's willing to work under compulsion is too dangerous a brute to entrust with a job in the stockyards—never occurred to those who proposed to help the sick by making life impossible for the healthy. I have often wondered at the smugness with which people assert their right to enslave me, to control my work, to force my will, to violate my conscience, to stifle my mind—yet what is it that they expect to depend on, when they lie on an operating table under my hands? Their moral code has taught them to believe that it is safe to rely on the virtue of their victims. Well, that is the virtue I have withdrawn. Let them discover the kind of doctors that their system will now produce. Let them discover, in their operating rooms and hospital wards, that it is not safe to place their lives in the hands of a man whose life they have throttled. It is not safe, if he is the sort of man who resents it—and still less safe, if he is the sort who doesn't."

THE NATURE OF AN ARTIST

This is an excerpt from a conversation between Dagny Taggart, the heroine of the story, and Richard Halley, a great composer, who is now on strike.

"Miss Taggart, how many people are there to whom my work means as much as it does to you?... That is the payment I demand. Not many can afford it. I don't mean your enjoyment, I don't mean your emotion—emotions be damned!—I mean your *understanding* and the fact that your enjoyment was of the same nature as mine, that it came from the same source: from your intelligence, from the conscious judgment of a mind able to judge my work by the standard of the same values that went to write it—I mean, not the fact that you *felt*, but that you felt what *I* wished you to feel, not the fact that you admire my work, but that you admire it for the things *I* wished to be admired.... There's only one passion in most artists more violent than their desire for admiration: their fear of identifying the nature of such admiration as they do receive. But it's a fear I've never shared. I do not fool myself about my work or the response I seek—I value both too highly. I do not care to be admired causelessly, emotionally, intuitively, instinctively—or blindly. I do not care for blindness in any form, I have too much to show—or for deafness, I have too much to say. I do not care to be admired by anyone's *heart*—only by someone's *head*. And when I find a customer with that invaluable capacity, then my performance is a mutual trade to mutual profit. An artist is a trader, Miss Taggart, the hardest and most exacting of all traders....

"Do you see why I'd give three dozen modern artists for one real businessman?... Whether it's a symphony or a coal mine, all work is an act of creating and comes from the same source: from an inviolate capacity to see through one's own eyes—which means: the capacity to perform a rational identification—which means: the capacity to see, to connect and to make what had not been seen, connected and made before. That shining vision which they talk about as belonging to the authors of symphonies and novels—what do they think is the driving faculty of men who discover how to use oil, how to run a mine, how to build an electric motor? That sacred fire which is said to burn within musicians and poets—what do they suppose moves an industrialist to defy the whole world for the sake of his new metal, as the inventors of the airplane, the builders of the railroads, the discoverers of new germs or new continents have done through all the ages?... An intransigent devotion

to the pursuit of truth, Miss Taggart? Have you heard the
moralists and the art lovers of the centuries talk about the
artist's intransigent devotion to the pursuit of truth? Name
me a greater example of such devotion than the act of a
man who says that the earth does turn, or the act of a man
who says that an alloy of steel and copper has certain
properties which enable it to do certain things, that it *is* and
does—and let the world rack him or ruin him, he will not
bear false witness to the evidence of his mind! *This*, Miss
Taggart, this sort of spirit, courage and love for truth—as
against a sloppy bum who goes around proudly assuring you
that he has almost reached the perfection of a lunatic, because he's an artist who hasn't the faintest idea what his
art work is or means, he's not restrained by such crude
concepts as 'being' or 'meaning,' he's the vehicle of higher
mysteries, he doesn't know how he created his work or
why, it just came out of him spontaneously, like vomit out
of a drunkard, he did not think, he wouldn't stoop to thinking, he just *felt* it, all he has to do is feel—he *feels*, the
flabby, loose-mouthed, shifty-eyed, drooling, shivering, un-
congealed bastard! I, who know what discipline, what effort, what tension of mind, what unrelenting strain upon
one's power of clarity are needed to produce a work of art—
I, who know that it requires a labor which makes a chain
gang look like rest and a severity no army-drilling sadist
could impose—I'll take the operator of a coal mine over
any walking vehicle of higher mysteries. The operator knows
that it's not his feelings that keep the coal carts moving
under the earth—and he knows what does keep them moving. Feelings? Oh yes, we do feel, he, you and I—we are,
in fact, the only people capable of feeling—and we know
where our feelings come from. But what we did not know
and have delayed learning for too long is the nature of those
who claim that they cannot account for their feelings. We
did not know what it is that they feel. We are learning
it now. It was a costly error. And those most guilty of it,
will pay the hardest price—as, in justice, they must. Those
most guilty of it were the real artists, who will now see
that they are first to be exterminated and that they had
prepared the triumph of their own exterminators by helping
to destroy their only protectors. For if there is more tragic
a fool than the businessman who doesn't know that he's an

exponent of man's highest creative spirit—it's the artist who thinks that the businessman is his enemy."

"THIS IS JOHN GALT SPEAKING"

This is the philosophy of Objectivism.

"Ladies and gentlemen," said a voice that came from the radio receiver—a man's clear, calm, implacable voice, the kind of voice that had not been heard on the airwaves for years—"Mr. Thompson will not speak to you tonight. His time is up. I have taken it over. You were to hear a report on the world crisis. That is what you are going to hear. . . .

"For twelve years, you have been asking: Who is John Galt? This is John Galt speaking. I am the man who loves his life. I am the man who does not sacrifice his love or his values. I am the man who has deprived you of victims and thus has destroyed your world, and if you wish to know why you are perishing—you who dread knowledge—I am the man who will now tell you. . . .

"You have heard it said that this is an age of moral crisis. You have said it yourself, half in fear, half in hope that the words had no meaning. You have cried that man's sins are destroying the world and you have cursed human nature for its unwillingness to practice the virtues you demanded. Since virtue, to you, consists of sacrifice, you have demanded more sacrifices at every successive disaster. In the name of a return to morality, you have sacrificed all those evils which you held as the cause of your plight. You have sacrificed justice to mercy. You have sacrificed independence to unity. You have sacrificed reason to faith. You have sacrificed wealth to need. You have sacrificed self-esteem to self-denial. You have sacrificed happiness to duty.

"You have destroyed all that which you held to be evil and achieved all that which you held to be good. Why, then, do you shrink in horror from the sight of the world around you? That world is not the product of your sins, it is the product and the image of your virtues. It is your moral ideal brought into reality in its full and final perfection. You have fought for it, you have dreamed of it, you have wished it, and I—I am the man who has granted you your wish.

"Your ideal had an implacable enemy, which your code of morality was designed to destroy. I have withdrawn that enemy. I have taken it out of your way and out of your reach. I have removed the source of all those evils you were sacrificing one by one. I have ended your battle. I have stopped your motor. I have deprived your world of man's mind.

"Men do not live by the mind, you say? I have withdrawn those who do. The mind is impotent, you say? I have withdrawn those whose mind isn't. There are values higher than the mind, you say? I have withdrawn those for whom there aren't.

"While you were dragging to your sacrificial altars the men of justice, of independence, of reason, of wealth, of self-esteem—I beat you to it, I reached them first. I told them the nature of the game you were playing and the nature of that moral code of yours, which they had been too innocently generous to grasp. I showed them the way to live by another morality—mine. It is mine that they chose to follow.

"All the men who have vanished, the men you hated, yet dreaded to lose, it is I who have taken them away from you. Do not attempt to find us. We do not choose to be found. Do not cry that it is our duty to serve you. We do not recognize such duty. Do not cry that you need us. We do not consider need a claim. Do not cry that you own us. You don't. Do not beg us to return. We are on strike, we, the men of the mind.

"We are on strike against self-immolation. We are on strike against the creed of unearned rewards and unrewarded duties. We are on strike against the dogma that the pursuit of one's happiness is evil. We are on strike against the doctrine that life is guilt.

"There is a difference between our strike and all those you've practiced for centuries: our strike consists, not of making demands, but of granting them. We are evil, according to your morality. We have chosen not to harm you any longer. We are useless, according to your economics. We have chosen not to exploit you any longer. We are dangerous and to be shackled, according to your politics. We have chosen not to endanger you, nor to wear the shackles any longer. We are only an illusion, according to your philosophy. We have chosen not to blind you any longer and have left you free to face reality—the reality you wanted, the world as you see it now, a world without mind.

"We have granted you everything you demanded of us, we who had always been the givers, but have only now understood it. We have no demands to present to you, no terms to bargain about, no compromise to reach. You have nothing to offer us. *We do not need you.*

"Are you now crying: No, this was not what you wanted? A mindless world of ruins was not your goal? You did not want us to leave you? You moral cannibals, I know that you've always known what it was that you wanted. But your game is up, because *now* we know it, too.

"Through centuries of scourges and disasters, brought about by your code of morality, you have cried that your code had been broken, that the scourges were punishment for breaking it, that men were too weak and too selfish to spill all the blood it required. You damned man, you damned existence, you damned this earth, but never dared to question your code. Your victims took the blame and struggled on, with your curses as reward for their martyrdom—while you went on crying that your code was noble, but human nature was not good enough to practice it. And no one rose to ask the question: Good?—by what standard?

"You wanted to know John Galt's identity. I am the man who has asked that question.

"Yes, this *is* an age of moral crisis. Yes, you *are* bearing punishment for your evil. But it is not man who is now on trial and it is not human nature that will take the blame. It is your moral code that's through, this time. Your moral code has reached its climax, the blind alley at the end of its course. And if you wish to go on living, what you now need is not to *return* to morality—you who have never known any—but to *discover* it.

"You have heard no concepts of morality but the mystical or the social. You have been taught that morality is a code of behavior imposed on you by whim, the whim of a supernatural power or the whim of society, to serve God's purpose or your neighbor's welfare, to please an authority beyond the grave or else next door—but not to serve *your* life or pleasure. Your pleasure, you have been taught, is to be found in immorality, your interests would best be served by evil, and any moral code must be designed not *for* you, but *against* you, not to further your life, but to drain it.

"For centuries, the battle of morality was fought between those who claimed that your life belongs to God and those who claimed that it belongs to your neighbors—between those who preached that the good is self-sacrifice for the sake of ghosts in heaven and those who preached that the good is self-sacrifice for the sake of incompetents on earth. And no one came to say that your life belongs to you and that the good is to live it.

"Both sides agreed that morality demands the surrender of your self-interest and of your mind, that the moral and the practical are opposites, that morality is not the province of reason, but the province of faith and force. Both sides agreed that no rational morality is possible, that there is no right or wrong in reason—that in reason there's no reason to be moral.

"Whatever else they fought about, it was against man's mind that all your moralists have stood united. It was man's mind that all their schemes and systems were intended to despoil and destroy. Now choose to perish or to learn that the anti-mind is the anti-life.

"Man's mind is his basic tool of survival. Life is given to him, survival is not. His body is given to him, its sustenance is not. His mind is given to him, its content is not. To remain alive, he must act, and before he can act he must know the nature and purpose of his action. He cannot obtain his food without a knowledge of food and of the way to obtain it. He cannot dig a ditch—or build a cyclotron—without a knowledge of his aim and of the means to achieve it. To remain alive, he must think.

"But to think is an act of choice. The key to what you so recklessly call 'human nature,' the open secret you live with, yet dread to name, is the fact that *man is a being of volitional consciousness*. Reason does not work automatically; thinking is not a mechanical process; the connections of logic are not made by instinct. The function of your stomach, lungs or heart is automatic; the function of your mind is not. In any hour and issue of your life, you are free to think or to evade that effort. But you are not free to escape from your nature, from the fact that *reason* is your means of survival—so that for *you*, who are a human being, the question 'to be or not to be' is the question 'to think or not to think.'

"A being of volitional consciousness has no automatic

course of behavior. He needs a code of values to guide his actions. 'Value' is that which one acts to gain and keep, 'virtue' is the action by which one gains and keeps it. 'Value' presupposes an answer to the question: of value to whom and for what? 'Value' presupposes a standard, a purpose and the necessity of action in the face of an alternative. Where there are no alternatives, no values are possible.

"There is only one fundamental alternative in the universe: existence or non-existence—and it pertains to a single class of entities: to living organisms. The existence of inanimate matter is unconditional, the existence of life is not: it depends on a specific course of action. Matter is indestructible, it changes its forms, but it cannot cease to exist. It is only a living organism that faces a constant alternative: the issue of life or death. Life is a process of self-sustaining and self-generated action. If an organism fails in that action, it dies; its chemical elements remain, but its life goes out of existence. It is only the concept of 'Life' that makes the concept of 'Value' possible. It is only to a living entity that things can be good or evil.

"A plant must feed itself in order to live; the sunlight, the water, the chemicals it needs are the values its nature has set it to pursue; its life is the standard of value directing its actions. But a plant has no choice of action; there are alternatives in the conditions it encounters, but there is no alternative in its function: it acts automatically to further its life, it cannot act for its own destruction.

"An animal is equipped for sustaining its life; its senses provide it with an automatic code of action, an automatic knowledge of what is good for it or evil. It has no power to extend its knowledge or to evade it. In conditions where its knowledge proves inadequate, it dies. But so long as it lives, it acts on its knowledge, with automatic safety and no power of choice, it is unable to ignore its own good, unable to decide to choose the evil and act as its own destroyer.

"Man has no automatic code of survival. His particular distinction from all other living species is the necessity to act in the face of alternatives by means of *volitional choice*. He has no automatic knowledge of what is good for him or evil, what values his life depends on, what course of action it requires. Are you prattling about an instinct of self-preservation? An *instinct* of self-preservation is precisely what man does not possess. An 'instinct' is an unerring and automatic form of knowledge. A desire is not an instinct. A desire to live does not give you the knowledge required for living. And even man's desire to live is not automatic: your secret evil today is that *that* is the desire you do not hold. Your fear of death is not a love for life and will not give you the knowledge needed to keep it. Man must obtain his knowledge and choose his actions by a process of thinking, which nature will not force him to perform. Man has the power to act as his own destroyer—and that is the way he has acted through most of his history.

"A living entity that regarded its means of survival as evil, would not survive. A plant that struggled to mangle its roots, a bird that fought to break its wings would not remain for long in the existence they affronted. But the history of man has been a struggle to deny and to destroy his mind.

"Man has been called a rational being, but rationality is a matter of choice—and the alternative his nature offers him is: rational being or suicidal animal. Man has to be man—by choice; he has to hold his life as a value—by choice; he has to learn to sustain it—by choice; he has to discover the values it requires and practice his virtues—by choice.

"A code of values accepted by choice is a code of morality.

"Whoever you are, you who are hearing me now, I am speaking to whatever living remnant is left uncorrupted within you, to the remnant of the human, to your *mind*, and I say: There *is* a morality of reason, a morality proper to man, and *Man's Life* is its standard of value.

"All that which is proper to the life of a rational being is the good; all that which destroys it is the evil.

"Man's life, as required by his nature, is not the life of a mindless brute, of a looting thug or a mooching mystic, but the life of a thinking being—not life by means of force or fraud, but life by means of achievement—not survival at any price, since there's only one price that pays for man's survival: reason.

"Man's life is the *standard* of morality, but your own life is its *purpose*. If existence on earth is your goal, you must choose your actions and values by the standard of that which is proper to man—for the purpose of preserving, fulfilling and enjoying the irreplaceable value which is your life.

"Since life requires a specific course of action, any other course will destroy it. A being who does not hold his own life as the motive and goal of his actions, is acting on the motive and standard of *death*. Such a being is a metaphysical monstrosity, struggling to oppose, negate and contradict the fact of his own existence, running blindly amuck on a trail of destruction, capable of nothing but pain.

"Happiness is the successful state of life, pain is an agent of death. Happiness is that state of consciousness which proceeds from the achievement of one's values. A morality that dares to tell you to find happiness in the renunciation of your happiness—to value the failure of your values—is an insolent negation of morality. A doctrine that gives you, as an ideal, the role of a sacrificial animal seeking slaughter on the altars of others, is giving you *death* as your standard. By the grace of reality and the nature of life, man—every man —is an end in himself, he exists for his own sake, and the achievement of his own happiness is his highest moral purpose.

"But neither life nor happiness can be achieved by the pursuit of irrational whims. Just as man is free to attempt to survive in any random manner, but will perish unless he lives as his nature requires, so he is free to seek his happiness in any mindless fraud, but the torture of frustration is all he will find, unless he seeks the happiness proper to man. The purpose of morality is to teach you, not to suffer and die, but to enjoy yourself and live.

"Sweep aside those parasites of subsidized classrooms, who live on the profits of the mind of others and proclaim that man needs no morality, no values, no code of behavior. They, who pose as scientists and claim that man is only an animal, do not grant him inclusion in the law of existence they have granted to the lowest of insects. They recognize that every living species has a way of survival demanded by its nature, they do not claim that a fish can live out of water or that a dog can live without its sense of smell—but man, they claim, the most complex of beings, man can survive in any way whatever, man has no identity, no nature, and there's no practical reason why he cannot live with his means of survival destroyed, with his mind throttled and placed at the disposal of any orders *they* might care to issue.

"Sweep aside those hatred-eaten mystics, who pose as friends of humanity and preach that the highest virtue man can practice is to hold his own life as of no value. Do they tell you that the purpose of morality is to curb man's instinct of self-preservation? It is for the purpose of self-preservation that man needs a code of morality. The only man who desires to be moral is the man who desires to live.

"No, you do not have to live; it is your basic act of choice; but if you choose to live, you must live as a man—by the work and the judgment of your mind.

"No, you do not have to live as a man; it is an act of moral choice. But you cannot live as anything else—and the alternative is that state of living death which you now see within you and around you, the state of a thing unfit for existence, no longer human and less than animal, a thing that knows nothing but pain and drags itself through its span of years in the agony of unthinking self-destruction.

"No, you do not have to think; it is an act of moral choice. But someone had to think to keep you alive; if you choose to default, you default on existence and you pass the deficit to some moral man, expecting him to sacrifice his good for the sake of letting you survive by your evil.

"No, you do not have to be a man; but today those who are, are not there any longer. I have removed your means of survival—your victims.

"If you wish to know how I have done it and what I told them to make them quit, you are hearing it now. I told them, in essence, the statement I am making tonight. They were men who had lived by my code, but had not known how great a virtue it represented. I made them see it. I brought them, not a re-evaluation, but only an identification of their values.

"We, the men of the mind, are now on strike against you in the name of a single axiom, which is the root of our moral code, just as the root of yours is the wish to escape it: the axiom that *existence exists*.

"Existence exists—and the act of grasping that statement implies two corollary axioms: that something exists which one perceives and that one exists possessing consciousness, consciousness being the faculty of perceiving that which exists.

"If nothing exists, there can be no consciousness: a consciousness with nothing to be conscious of is a contradiction in terms. A consciousness conscious of nothing but itself is a contradiction in terms: before it could identify itself as consciousness, it had to be conscious of something. If that which you claim to perceive does not exist, what you possess is not consciousness.

"Whatever the degree of your knowledge, these two—existence and consciousness—are axioms you cannot escape, these two are the irreducible primaries implied in any action you undertake, in any part of your knowledge and in its sum, from the first ray of light you perceive at the start of your life to the widest erudition you might acquire at its end. Whether you know the shape of a pebble or the structure of a solar system, the axioms remain the same: that *it* exists and that you *know* it.

"To exist is to be something, as distinguished from the nothing of non-existence, it is to be an entity of a specific nature made of specific attributes. Centuries ago, the man who was—no matter what his errors—the greatest of your philosophers, has stated the formula defining the concept of existence and the rule of all knowledge: *A is A*. A thing is itself. You have never grasped the meaning of his statement. I am here to complete it: Existence is Identity, Consciousness is Identification.

"Whatever you choose to consider, be it an object, an attribute or an action, the law of identity remains the same. A leaf cannot be a stone at the same time, it cannot be all red and all green at the same time, it cannot freeze and burn at the same time. A is A. Or, if you wish it stated in simpler language: You cannot have your cake and eat it, too.

"Are you seeking to know what is wrong with the world? All the disasters that have wrecked your world, came from your leaders' attempt to evade the fact that A is A. All the secret evil you dread to face within you and all the pain you have ever endured, came from your own attempt to evade the fact that A is A. The purpose of those who taught you to evade it, was to make you forget that Man is Man.

"Man cannot survive except by gaining knowledge, and reason is his only means to gain it. Reason is the faculty that perceives, identifies and integrates the material provided by his senses. The task of his senses is to give him the evidence of existence, but the task of identifying it belongs to his reason, his senses tell him only that something *is*, but *what* it is must be learned by his mind.

"All thinking is a process of identification and integration. Man perceives a blob of color; by integrating the evidence of his sight and his touch, he learns to identify it as a solid object; he learns to identify the object as a table; he learns that the table is made of wood; he learns that the wood consists of cells, that the cells consist of molecules, that the molecules consist of atoms. All through this process, the work of his mind consists of answers to a single question: *What* is it? His means to establish the truth of his answers is logic, and logic rests on the axiom that existence exists. Logic is the art of *non-contradictory identification*. A contradiction cannot exist. An atom is itself, and so is the universe; neither can contradict its own identity; nor can a part contradict the whole. No concept man forms is valid unless he integrates it without contradiction into the total sum of his knowledge. To arrive at a contradiction is to confess an error in one's thinking; to maintain a contradiction is to abdicate one's mind and to evict oneself from the realm of reality.

"Reality is that which exists; the unreal does not exist; the unreal is merely that negation of existence which is the content of a human consciousness when it attempts to abandon reason. Truth is the recognition of reality; reason, man's only means of knowledge, is his only standard of truth.

"The most depraved sentence you can now utter is to ask: *Whose* reason? The answers is: *Yours*. No matter how vast your knowledge or how modest, it is your own mind that has to acquire it. It is only with your own knowledge that you can deal. It is only your own knowledge that you can claim to possess or ask others to consider. Your mind is your only judge of truth—and if others dissent from your verdict, reality is the court of final appeal. Nothing but a man's mind can perform that complex, delicate, crucial process of identification which is thinking. Nothing can direct the process but his own judgment. Nothing can direct his judgment but his moral integrity.

"You who speak of a 'moral instinct' as if it were some separate endowment opposed to reason—man's reason *is* his moral faculty. A process of reason is a process of constant choice in answer to the question: True or False?—*Right or Wrong?* Is a seed to be planted in soil in order to grow—right or wrong? Is a man's wound to be disinfected in order to save his life—right or wrong? Does the nature of atmospheric electricity permit it to be converted into kinetic power—right or wrong? It is the answers to such questions that gave you everything you have—and the answers came from a man's mind, a mind of intransigent devotion to that which is *right*.

"A rational process is a *moral* process. You may make an

error at any step of it, with nothing to protect you but your own severity, or you may try to cheat, to fake the evidence and evade the effort of the quest—but if devotion to truth is the hallmark of morality, then there is no greater, nobler, more heroic form of devotion than the act of a man who assumes the responsibility of thinking.

"That which you call your soul or spirit is your consciousness, and that which you call 'free will' is your mind's freedom to think or not, the only will you have, your only freedom, the choice that controls all the choices you make and determines your life and your character.

"Thinking is man's only basic virtue, from which all the others proceed. And his basic vice, the source of all his evils, is that nameless act which all of you practice, but struggle never to admit: the act of blanking out, the willful suspension of one's consciousness, the refusal to think—not blindness, but the refusal to see; not ignorance, but the refusal to know. It is the act of unfocusing your mind and inducing an inner fog to escape the responsibility of judgment—on the unstated premise that a thing will not exist if only you refuse to identify it, that A will not be A so long as you do not pronounce the verdict 'It *is*.' Non-thinking is an act of annihilation, a wish to negate existence, an attempt to wipe out reality. But existence exists; reality is not to be wiped out, it will merely wipe out the wiper. By refusing to say 'It is,' you are refusing to say 'I am.' By suspending your judgment, you are negating your person. When a man declares: 'Who am I to know?'—he is declaring: 'Who am I to live?'

"This, in every hour and every issue, is your basic moral choice: thinking or non-thinking, existence or non-existence, A or non-A, entity or zero.

"To the extent to which a man is rational, life is the premise directing his actions. To the extent to which he is irrational, the premise directing his actions is death.

"You who prattle that morality is social and that man would need no morality on a desert island—it is on a desert island that he would need it most. Let him try to claim, when there are no victims to pay for it, that a rock is a house, that sand is clothing, that food will drop into his mouth without cause or effort, that he will collect a harvest tomorrow by devouring his stock seed today—and reality will wipe him out, as he deserves; reality will show him that life is a value to be bought and that thinking is the only coin noble enough to buy it.

"If I were to speak your kind of language, I would say that man's only moral commandment is: Thou shalt think. But a 'moral commandment' is a contradiction in terms. The moral is the chosen, not the forced; the understood, not the obeyed. The moral is the rational, and reason accepts no commandments.

"My morality, the morality of reason, is contained in a single axiom: existence exists—and in a single choice: to live. The rest proceeds from these. To live, man must hold three things as the supreme and ruling values of his life: Reason—Purpose—Self-esteem. Reason, as his only tool of knowledge—Purpose, as his choice of the happiness which that tool must proceed to achieve—Self-esteem, as his inviolate certainty that his mind is competent to think and his person is worthy of happiness, which means: is worthy of living. These three values imply and require all of man's virtues, and all his virtues pertain to the relation of existence and consciousness: rationality, independence, integrity, honesty, justice, productiveness, pride.

"Rationality is the recognition of the fact that existence exists, that nothing can alter the truth and nothing can take precedence over that act of perceiving it, which is thinking—that the mind is one's only judge of values and one's only guide of action—that reason is an absolute that permits no compromise—that a concession to the irrational invalidates one's consciousness and turns it from the task of perceiving to the task of faking reality—that the alleged short-cut to knowledge, which is faith, is only a short-circuit destroying the mind—that the acceptance of a mystical invention is a wish for the annihilation of existence and, properly, annihilates one's consciousness.

"Independence is the recognition of the fact that yours is the responsibility of judgment and nothing can help you escape it—that no substitute can do your thinking, as no pinch-hitter can live your life—that the vilest form of self-abasement and self-destruction is the subordination of your mind to the mind of another, the acceptance of an authority over your brain, the acceptance of his assertions as facts, his say-so as truth, his edicts as middle-man between your consciousness and your existence.

"Integrity is the recognition of the fact that you cannot

fake your consciousness, just as honesty is the recognition of
the fact that you cannot fake existence—that man is an indivisible entity, an integrated unit of two attributes: of matter and consciousness, and that he may permit no breach between body and mind, between action and thought, between
his life and his convictions—that, like a judge impervious to
public opinion, he may not sacrifice his convictions to the
wishes of others, be it the whole of mankind shouting pleas
or threats against him—that courage and confidence are practical necessities, that courage is the practical form of being true to existence, of being true to truth, and confidence
is the practical form of being true to one's own consciousness.

"Honesty is the recognition of the fact that the unreal is
unreal and can have no value, that neither love nor fame nor
cash is a value if obtained by fraud—that an attempt to gain
a value by deceiving the mind of others is an act of raising
your victims to a position higher than reality, where you become a pawn of their blindness, a slave of their non-thinking
and their evasions, while their intelligence, their rationality,
their perceptiveness become the enemies you have to dread
and flee—that you do not care to live as a dependent, least
of all a dependent on the stupidity of others, or as a fool
whose source of values is the fools he succeeds in fooling—
that honesty is not a social duty, not a sacrifice for the sake
of others, but the most profoundly selfish virtue man can practice: his refusal to sacrifice the reality of his own existence
to the deluded consciousness of others.

"Justice is the recognition of the fact that you cannot
fake the character of men as you cannot fake the character
of nature, that you must judge all men as conscientiously as
you judge inanimate objects, with the same respect for truth,
with the same incorruptible vision, by as pure and as *rational* a process of identification—that every man must be
judged for what he *is* and treated accordingly, that just as
you do not pay a higher price for a rusty chunk of scrap than
for a piece of shining metal, so you do not value a rotter
above a hero—that your moral appraisal is the coin paying
men for their virtues or vices, and this payment demands of
you as scrupulous an honor as you bring to financial trans-
actions—that to withhold your contempt from men's vices is
an act of moral counterfeiting, and to withhold your admiration from their virtues is an act of moral embezzlement—that
to place any other concern higher than justice is to devaluate

your moral currency and defraud the good in favor of the
evil, since only the good can lose by a default of justice and
only the evil can profit—and that the bottom of the pit at the
end of that road, the act of moral bankruptcy, is to punish
men for their virtues and reward them for their vices, that
that is the collapse to full depravity, the Black Mass of the
worship of death, the dedication of your consciousness to the
destruction of existence.

"Productiveness is your acceptance of morality, your recognition of the fact that you choose to live—that productive
work is the process by which man's consciousness controls
his existence, a constant process of acquiring knowledge
and shaping matter to fit one's purpose, of translating an
idea into physical form, of remaking the earth in the image
of one's values—that *all* work is creative work if done by
a thinking mind, and no work is creative if done by a blank
who repeats in uncritical stupor a routine he has learned
from others—that your work is yours to choose, and the
choice is as wide as your mind, that nothing more is possible to you and nothing less is human—that to cheat your
way into a job bigger than your mind can handle is to become a fear-corroded ape on borrowed motions and borrowed time, and to settle down into a job that requires less
than your mind's full capacity is to cut your motor and sentence yourself to another kind of motion: decay—that your
work is the process of achieving your values, and to lose
your ambition for values is to lose your ambition to live—
that your body is a machine, but your mind is its driver,
and you must drive as far as your mind will take you, with
achievement as the goal of your road—that the man who
has no purpose is a machine that coasts downhill at the
mercy of any boulder to crash in the first chance ditch, that
the man who stifles his mind is a stalled machine slowly
going to rust, that the man who lets a leader prescribe his
course is a wreck being towed to the scrap heap, and the
man who makes another man his goal is a hitchhiker no
driver should ever pick up—that your work is the purpose
of your life, and you must speed past any killer who assumes the right to stop you, that any value you might find
outside your work, any other loyalty or love, can be only
travelers you choose to share your journey and must be
travelers going on their own power in the same direction.

"Pride is the recognition of the fact that you are your own

highest value and, like all of man's values, it has to be earned—that of any achievements open to you, the one that makes all others possible is the creation of your own character—that your character, your actions, your desires, your emotions are the products of the premises held by your mind—that as man must produce the physical values he needs to sustain his life, so he must acquire the values of character that make his life worth sustaining—that as man is a being of self-made wealth, so he is a being of self-made soul—that to live requires a sense of self-value, but man, who has no automatic values, has no automatic sense of self-esteem and must earn it by shaping his soul in the image of his moral ideal, in the image of Man, the rational being he is born able to create, but must create by choice—that the first precondition of self-esteem is that radiant selfishness of soul which desires the best in all things, in values of matter and spirit, a soul that seeks above all else to achieve its own moral perfection, valuing nothing higher than itself—and that the proof of an achieved self-esteem is your soul's shudder of contempt and rebellion against the role of a sacrificial animal, against the vile impertinence of any creed that proposes to immolate the irreplaceable value which is your consciousness and the incomparable glory which is your existence to the blind evasions and the stagnant decay of others.

"Are you beginning to see who is John Galt? I am the man who has earned the thing you did not fight for, the thing you have renounced, betrayed, corrupted, yet were unable fully to destroy and are now hiding as your guilty secret, spending your life in apologies to every professional cannibal, lest it be discovered that somewhere within you, you still long to say what I am now saying to the hearing of the whole of mankind: I am proud of my own value and of the fact that I wish to live.

"This wish—which you share, yet submerge as an evil—is the only remnant of the good within you, but it is a wish one must learn to deserve. His own happiness is man's only moral purpose, but only his own virtue can achieve it. Virtue is not an end in itself. Virtue is not its own reward or sacrificial fodder for the reward of evil. *Life* is the reward of virtue—and happiness is the goal and the reward of life.

"Just as your body has two fundamental sensations, pleasure and pain, as signs of its welfare or injury, as a barometer of its basic alternative, life or death, so your consciousness has two fundamental emotions, joy and suffering, in answer to the same alternative. Your emotions are estimates of that which furthers your life or threatens it, lightning calculators giving you a sum of your profit or loss. You have no choice about your capacity to feel that something is good for you or evil, but *what* you will consider good or evil, what will give you joy or pain, what you will love or hate, desire or fear, depends on your standard of value. Emotions are inherent in your nature, but their content is dictated by your mind. Your emotional capacity is an empty motor, and your values are the fuel with which your mind fills it. If you choose a mix of contradictions, it will clog your motor, corrode your transmission and wreck you on your first attempt to move with a machine which you, the driver, have corrupted.

"If you hold the irrational as your standard of value and the impossible as your concept of the good, if you long for rewards you have not earned, for a fortune or a love you don't deserve, for a loophole in the law of causality, for an A that becomes non-A at your whim, if you desire the opposite of existence—you will reach it. Do not cry, when you reach it, that life is frustration and that happiness is impossible to man; check your fuel: it brought you where you wanted to go.

"Happiness is not to be achieved at the command of emotional whims. Happiness is not the satisfaction of whatever irrational wishes you might blindly attempt to indulge. Happiness is a state of non-contradictory joy—a joy without penalty or guilt, a joy that does not clash with any of your values and does not work for your own destruction, not the joy of escaping from your mind, but of using your mind's fullest power, not the joy of faking reality, but of achieving values that are real; not the joy of a drunkard, but of a producer. Happiness is possible only to a rational man, the man who desires nothing but rational goals, seeks nothing but rational values and finds his joy in nothing but rational actions.

"Just as I support my life, neither by robbery nor alms, but by my own effort, so I do not seek to derive my happiness from the injury or the favor of others, but earn it by my own achievement. Just as I do not consider the pleasure of others as the goal of my life, so I do not consider my pleasure as the goal of the lives of others. Just as there are no contradictions in my values and no conflicts among my desires—so there are no victims and no conflicts of interest among rational men, men who do not desire the unearned and do not view one another with a cannibal's lust, men who neither make sacrifices nor accept them.

"The symbol of all relationships among such men, the moral symbol of respect for human beings, is *the trader*. We, who live by values, not by loot, are traders, both in matter and in spirit. A trader is a man who earns what he gets and does not give or take the undeserved. A trader does not ask to be paid for his failures, nor does he ask to be loved for his flaws. A trader does not squander his body as fodder or his soul as alms. Just as he does not give his work except in trade for material values, so he does not give the values of his spirit—his love, his friendship, his esteem—except in payment and in trade for human virtues, in payment for his own selfish pleasure, which he receives from men he can respect. The mystic parasites who have, throughout the ages, reviled the traders and held them in contempt, while honoring the beggars and the looters, have known the secret motive of their sneers: a trader is the entity they dread—a man of justice.

"Do you ask what moral obligation I owe to my fellow men? None—except the obligation I owe to myself, to material objects and to all of existence: rationality. I deal with men as my nature and theirs demands: by means of reason. I seek or desire nothing from them except such relations as they care to enter of their own voluntary choice. It is only with their mind that I can deal and only for my own self-interest, when they see that my interest coincides with theirs. When they don't, I enter no relationship; I let dissenters go their way and I do not swerve from mine. I win by means of nothing but logic and I surrender to nothing but logic. I do not surrender my reason or deal with men who surrender theirs. I have nothing to gain from fools or cowards; I have no benefits to seek from human vices: from stupidity, dishonesty or fear. The only value men can offer me is the work of their mind. When I disagree with a rational man, I let reality be our final arbiter; if I am right, he will learn; if I am wrong, I will; one of us will win, but both will profit.

"Whatever may be open to disagreement, there is one act of evil that may not, the act that no man may commit against others and no man may sanction or forgive. So long as men desire to live together, no man may *initiate*—do you hear me? no man may *start*—the use of physical force against others.

"To interpose the threat of physical destruction between a man and his perception of reality, is to negate and paralyze his means of survival; to force him to act against his own judgment, is like forcing him to act against his own sight. Whoever, to whatever purpose or extent, initiates the use of force, is a killer acting on the premise of death in a manner wider than murder: the premise of destroying man's capacity to live.

"Do not open your mouth to tell me that your mind has convinced you of your right to force my mind. Force and mind are opposites; morality ends where a gun begins. When you declare that men are irrational animals and propose to treat them as such, you define thereby your own character and can no longer claim the sanction of reason—as no advocate of contradictions can claim it. There can be no 'right' to destroy the source of rights, the only means of judging right and wrong: the mind.

"To force a man to drop his own mind and to accept your will as a substitute, with a gun in place of a syllogism, with terror in place of proof, and death as the final argument—is to attempt to exist in defiance of reality. Reality demands of man that he act for his own rational interest; your gun demands of him that he act against it. Reality threatens man with death if he does not act on his rational judgment; you threaten him with death if he does. You place him in a world where the price of his life is the surrender of all the virtues required by life—and death by a process of gradual destruction is all that you and your system will achieve, when death is made to be the ruling power, the winning argument in a society of men.

"Be it a highwayman who confronts a traveler with the ultimatum: 'Your money or your life,' or a politician who confronts a country with the ultimatum: 'Your children's education or your life,' the meaning of that ultimatum is: 'Your mind or your life'—and neither is possible to man without the other.

"If there are degrees of evil, it is hard to say who is the more contemptible: the brute who assumes the right to force the mind of others or the moral degenerate who grants to others the right to force his mind. *That* is the moral absolute

one does not leave open to debate. I do not grant the terms of reason to men who propose to deprive me of reason. I do not enter discussions with neighbors who think they can forbid me to think. I do not place my moral sanction upon a murderer's wish to kill me. When a man attempts to deal with me by force, I answer him—by force.

"It is only as retaliation that force may be used and only against the man who starts its use. No, I do not share his evil or sink to his concept of morality: I merely grant him his choice, destruction, the only destruction he had the right to choose: his own. He uses force to seize a value; I use it only to destroy destruction. A holdup man seeks to gain wealth by killing me; I do not grow richer by killing a holdup man. I seek no values by means of evil, nor do I surrender my values to evil.

"In the name of all the producers who had kept you alive and received your death ultimatums in payment, I now answer you with a single ultimatum of our own: Our work or your guns. You can choose either; you can't have both. We do not initiate the use of force against others or submit to force at their hands. If you desire ever again to live in an industrial society, it will be on *our* moral terms. Our terms and our motive power are the antithesis of yours. You have been using fear as your weapon and have been bringing death to man as his punishment for rejecting your morality. We offer him life as his reward for accepting ours.

"You who are worshippers of the zero—you have never discovered that achieving life is not the equivalent of avoiding death. Joy is not 'the absence of pain,' intelligence is not 'the absence of stupidity,' light is not 'the absence of darkness,' an entity is not 'the absence of a nonentity.' Building is not done by abstaining from demolition; centuries of sitting and waiting in such abstinence will not raise one single girder for you to abstain from demolishing—and now you can no longer say to me, the builder; 'Produce, and feed us in exchange for our *not* destroying your production.' I am answering in the name of all your victims: Perish with and in your own void. Existence is not a negation of negatives. Evil, not value, is an absence and a negation, evil is impotent and has no power but that which we let it extort from us. Perish, because we have learned that a zero cannot hold a mortgage over life.

"You seek escape from pain. We seek the achievement of

happiness. You exist for the sake of avoiding punishment. We exist for the sake of earning rewards. Threats will not make us function; fear is not our incentive. It is not death that we wish to avoid, but life that we wish to live.

"You, who have lost the concept of the difference, you who claim that fear and joy are incentives of equal power—and secretly add that fear is the more 'practical'—you do not wish to live, and only fear of death still holds you to the existence you have damned. You dart in panic through the trap of your days, looking for the exit you have closed, running from a pursuer you dare not name to a terror you dare not acknowledge, and the greater your terror the greater your dread of the only act that could save you: thinking. The purpose of your struggle is not to know, not to grasp or name or hear the thing I shall now state to your hearing: that yours is the Morality of Death.

"Death is the standard of your values, death is your chosen goal, and you have to keep running, since there is no escape from the pursuer who is out to destroy you or from the knowledge that that pursuer is yourself. Stop running, for once—there is no place to run—stand naked, as you dread to stand, but as I see you, and take a look at what you dared to call a moral code.

"Damnation is the start of your morality, destruction is its purpose, means and end. Your code begins by damning man as evil, then demands that he practice a good which it defines as impossible for him to practice. It demands, as his first proof of virtue, that he accept his own depravity without proof. It demands that he start, not with a standard of value, but with a standard of evil, which is himself, by means of which he is then to define the good: the good is that which he is not.

"It does not matter who then becomes the profiteer on his renounced glory and tormented soul, a mystic God with some incomprehensible design or any passer-by whose rotting sores are held as some inexplicable claim upon him—it does not matter, the good is not for him to understand, his duty is to crawl through years of penance, atoning for the guilt of his existence to any stray collector of unintelligible debts, his only concept of a value is a zero: the good is that which is non-man.

"The name of this monstrous absurdity is Original Sin.

"A sin without volition is a slap at morality and an insolent contradiction in terms: that which is outside the possibility of choice is outside the province of morality. If man is evil by birth, he has no will, no power to change it; if he has no will, he can be neither good nor evil; a robot is amoral. To hold, as man's sin, a fact not open to his choice is a mockery of morality. To hold man's nature as his sin is a mockery of nature. To punish him for a crime he committed before he was born is a mockery of justice. To hold him guilty in a matter where no innocence exists is a mockery of reason. To destroy morality, nature, justice and reason by means of a single concept is a feat of evil hardly to be matched. Yet-*that* is the root of your code.

"Do not hide behind the cowardly evasion that man is born with free will, but with a 'tendency' to evil. A free will saddled with a tendency is like a game with loaded dice. It forces man to struggle through the effort of playing, to bear responsibility and pay for the game, but the decision is weighted in favor of a tendency that he had no power to escape. If the tendency is of his choice, he cannot possess it at birth; if it is not of his choice, his will is not free.

"What is the nature of the guilt that your teachers call his Original Sin? What are the evils man acquired when he fell from a state they consider perfection? Their myth declares that he ate the fruit of the tree of knowledge—he acquired a mind and became a rational being. It was the knowledge of good and evil—he became a moral being. He was sentenced to earn his bread by his labor—he became a productive being. He was sentenced to experience desire—he acquired the capacity of sexual enjoyment. The evils for which they damn him are reason, morality, creativeness, joy—all the cardinal values of his existence. It is not his vices that their myth of man's fall is designed to explain and condemn, it is not his errors that they hold as his guilt, but the essence of his nature as man. Whatever he was—that robot in the Garden of Eden, who existed without mind, without values, without labor, without love—he was not man.

"Man's fall, according to your teachers, was that he gained the virtues required to live. These virtues, by their standard, are his Sin. His evil, they charge, is that he's man. His guilt, they charge, is that he lives.

"They call it a morality of mercy and a doctrine of love for man.

"No, they say, they do not preach that man is evil, the

evil is only that alien object: his body. No, they say, they do not wish to kill him, they only wish to make him lose his body. They seek to help him, they say, against his pain—and they point at the torture rack to which they've tied him, the rack with two wheels that pull him in opposite directions, the rack of the doctrine that splits his soul and body.

"They have cut man in two, setting one half against the other. They have taught him that his body and his consciousness are two enemies engaged in deadly conflict, two antagonists of opposite natures, contradictory claims, incompatible needs, that to benefit one is to injure the other, that his soul belongs to a supernatural realm, but his body is an evil prison holding it in bondage to this earth—and that the good is to defeat his body, to undermine it by years of patient struggle, digging his way to that glorious jail-break which leads into the freedom of the grave.

"They have taught man that he is a hopeless misfit made of two elements, both symbols of death. A body without a soul is a corpse, a soul without a body is a ghost—yet such is their image of man's nature: the battleground of a struggle between a corpse and a ghost, a corpse endowed with some evil volition of its own and a ghost endowed with the knowledge that everything known to man is non-existent, that only the unknowable exists.

"Do you observe what human faculty that doctrine was designed to ignore? It was man's mind that had to be negated in order to make him fall apart. Once he surrendered reason, he was left at the mercy of two monsters whom he could not fathom or control: of a body moved by unaccountable instincts and a soul moved by mystic revelations—he was left as the passively ravaged victim of a battle between a robot and a dictaphone.

"And as he now crawls through the wreckage, groping blindly for a way to live, your teachers offer him the help of a morality that proclaims that he'll find no solution and must seek no fulfillment on earth. Real existence, they tell him, is that which he cannot perceive, true consciousness is the faculty of perceiving the non-existent—and if he is unable to understand it, *that* is the proof that his existence is evil and his consciousness impotent.

"As products of the split between man's soul and body, there are two kinds of teachers of the Morality of Death: the mystics of spirit and the mystics of muscle, whom you call the spiritualists and the materialists, those who believe in consciousness without existence and those who believe in existence without consciousness. Both demand the surrender of your mind, one to their revelations, the other to their reflexes. No matter how loudly they posture in the roles of irreconcilable antagonists, their moral codes are alike, and so are their aims: in matter—the enslavement of man's body, in spirit—the destruction of his mind.

"The good, say the mystics of spirit, is God, a being whose only definition is that he is beyond man's power to conceive —a definition that invalidates man's consciousness and nullifies his concepts of existence. The good, say the mystics of muscle, is Society—a thing which they define as an organism that possesses no physical form, a super-being embodied in no one in particular and everyone in general except yourself. Man's mind, say the mystics of spirit, must be subordinated to the will of God. Man's mind, say the mystics of muscle, must be subordinated to the will of Society. Man's standard of value, say the mystics of spirit, is the pleasure of God, whose standards are beyond man's power of comprehension and must be accepted on faith. Man's standard of value, say the mystics of muscle, is the pleasure of Society, whose standards are beyond man's right of judgment and must be obeyed as a primary absolute. The purpose of man's life, say both, is to become an abject zombie who serves a purpose he does not know, for reasons he is not to question. His reward, say the mystics of spirit, will be given to him beyond the grave. His reward, say the mystics of muscle, will be given on earth—to his great-grandchildren.

"*Selfishness*—say both—is man's evil. Man's good—say both—is to give up his personal desires, to deny himself, renounce himself, surrender; man's good is to negate the life he lives. *Sacrifice*—cry both—is the essence of morality, the highest virtue within man's reach.

"Whoever is now within reach of my voice, whoever is man the victim, not man the killer, I am speaking at the deathbed of your mind, at the brink of that darkness in which you're drowning, and if there still remains within you the power to struggle to hold on to those fading sparks which had been yourself—use it now. The word that has destroyed you is '*sacrifice*.' Use the last of your strength to understand its meaning. You're still alive. You have a chance.

" 'Sacrifice' does not mean the rejection of the worthless,

but of the precious. 'Sacrifice' does not mean the rejection of
the evil for the sake of the good, but of the good for the
sake of the evil. 'Sacrifice' is the surrender of that which you
value in favor of that which you don't.

"If you exchange a penny for a dollar, it is *not* a sacrifice;
if you exchange a dollar for a penny, it *is*. If you achieve the
career you wanted, after years of struggle, it is *not* a sacrifice; if you then renounce it for the sake of a rival, it *is*. If
you own a bottle of milk and give it to your starving child,
it is *not* a sacrifice; if you give it to your neighbor's child
and let your own die, it *is*.

"If you give money to help a friend, it is *not* a sacrifice;
if you give it to a worthless stranger, it *is*. If you give your
friend a sum you can afford, it is *not* a sacrifice; if you
give him money at the cost of your own discomfort, it is
only a partial virtue, according to this sort of moral standard;
if you give him money at the cost of disaster to yourself—
that is the virtue of sacrifice in full.

"If you renounce all personal desires and dedicate your
life to those you love, you do not achieve full virtue: you
still retain a value of your own, which is your love. If you
devote your life to random strangers, it is an act of greater
virtue. If you devote your life to serving men you hate—*that*
is the greatest of the virtues you can practice.

"A sacrifice is the surrender of a value. Full sacrifice is full
surrender of all values. If you wish to achieve full virtue,
you must seek no gratitude in return for your sacrifice, no
praise, no love, no admiration, no self-esteem, not even the
pride of being virtuous; the faintest trace of any gain dilutes
your virtue. If you pursue a course of action that does
not taint your life by any joy, that brings you no value in
matter, no value in spirit, no gain, no profit, no reward—if
you achieve this state of total zero, you have achieved the
ideal of moral perfection.

"You are told that moral perfection is impossible to man
—and, by this standard it is. You cannot achieve it so long
as you live, but the value of your life and of your person is
gauged by how closely you succeed in approaching that ideal
zero which is *death*.

"If you start, however, as a passionless blank, as a vege-
table seeking to be eaten, with no values to reject and no
wishes to renounce, you will not win the crown of sacrifice.
It is not a sacrifice to renounce the unwanted. It is not a

sacrifice to give your life for others, if death is your personal desire. To achieve the virtue of sacrifice, you must want to live, you must love it, you must burn with passion for this earth and for all the splendor it can give you—you must feel the twist of every knife as it slashes your desires away from your reach and drains your love out of your body. It is not mere death that the morality of sacrifice holds out to you as an ideal, but death by slow torture.

"Do not remind me that it pertains only to this life on earth. I am concerned with no other. Neither are you.

"If you wish to save the last of your dignity, do not call your best actions a 'sacrifice': that term brands you as immoral. If a mother buys food for her hungry child rather than a hat for herself, it is *not* a sacrifice: she values the child higher than the hat; but it is a sacrifice to the kind of mother whose higher value is the hat, who would prefer her child to starve and feeds him only from a sense of duty. If a man dies fighting for his own freedom, it is *not* a sacrifice: he is not willing to live as a slave; but it *is* a sacrifice to the kind of man who's willing. If a man refuses to sell his convictions, it is *not* a sacrifice, unless he is the sort of man who has no convictions.

"Sacrifice could be proper only for those who have nothing to sacrifice—no values, no standards, no judgment—those whose desires are irrational whims, blindly conceived and lightly surrendered. For a man of moral stature, whose desires are born of rational values, sacrifice is the surrender of the right to the wrong, of the good to the evil.

"The creed of sacrifice is a morality for the immoral—a morality that declares its own bankruptcy by confessing that it can't impart to men any personal stake in virtues or values, and that their souls are sewers of depravity, which they must be taught to sacrifice. By its own confession, it is impotent to teach men to be good and can only subject them to constant punishment.

"Are you thinking, in some foggy stupor, that it's only *material* values that your morality requires you to sacrifice? And *what* do you think are material values? Matter has no value except as a means for the satisfaction of human desires. Matter is only a tool of human values. To what service are you asked to give the material tools your virtue has produced? To the service of that which *you* regard as evil: to a principle you do not share, to a person you do not respect, to the achievement of a purpose opposed to your own—else your gift is *not* a sacrifice.

"Your morality tells you to renounce the material world and to divorce your values from matter. A man whose values are given no expression in material form, whose existence is unrelated to his ideals, whose actions contradict his convictions, is a cheap little hypocrite—yet *that* is the man who obeys your morality and divorces his values from matter. The man who loves one woman, but sleeps with another —the man who admires the talent of a worker, but hires another—the man who considers one cause to be just, but donates his money to the support of another—the man who holds high standards of craftsmanship, but devotes his effort to the production of trash—*these* are the men who have renounced matter, the men who believe that the values of their spirit cannot be brought into material reality.

"Do you say it is the spirit that such men have renounced? Yes, of course. You cannot have one without the other. You are an indivisible entity of matter and consciousness. Renounce your consciousness and you become a brute. Renounce your body and you become a fake. Renounce the material world and you surrender it to evil.

"And *that* is precisely the goal of your morality, the duty that your code demands of you. Give to that which you do not enjoy, serve that which you do not admire, submit to that which you consider evil—surrender the world to the values of others, deny, reject, renounce your *self*. Your self is your *mind*; renounce it and you become a chunk of meat ready for any cannibal to swallow.

"It is your *mind* that they want you to surrender—all those who preach the creed of sacrifice, whatever their tags or their motives, whether they demand it for the sake of your soul or of your body, whether they promise you another life in heaven or a full stomach on this earth. Those who start by saying: 'It is selfish to pursue your own wishes, you must sacrifice them to the wishes of others'—end up by saying: 'It is selfish to uphold your convictions, you must sacrifice them to the convictions of others.'

"This much is true: the most *selfish* of all things is the independent mind that recognizes no authority higher than its own and no value higher than its judgment of truth. You are asked to sacrifice your intellectual integrity, your logic, your reason, your standard of truth—in favor of becoming a prostitute whose standard is the greatest good for the greatest number.

"If you search your code for guidance, for an answer to the question: 'What *is* the good?'—the only answer you will find is *'The good of others.'* The good is whatever others wish, whatever you feel they feel they wish, or whatever you feel they ought to feel. 'The good of others' is a magic formula that transforms anything into gold, a formula to be recited as a guarantee of moral glory and as a fumigator for any action, even the slaughter of a continent. Your standard of virtue is not an object, not an act, not a principle, but an *intention.* You need no proof, no reasons, no success, you need not achieve *in fact* the good of others—all you need to know is that your motive was the good of others, *not* your own. Your only definition of the good is a negation: the good is the 'non-good for me.'

"Your code—which boasts that it upholds eternal, absolute, objective moral values and scorns the conditional, the relative and the subjective—your code hands out, as its version of the absolute, the following rule of moral conduct: If *you* wish it, it's evil; if others wish it, it's good; if the motive of your action is *your* welfare, don't do it; if the motive is the welfare of others, then anything goes.

"As this double-jointed, double-standard morality splits you in half, so it splits mankind into two enemy camps: one is *you,* the other is all the rest of humanity. *You* are the only outcast who has no right to wish or live. *You* are the only servant, the rest are the masters, *you* are the only giver, the rest are the takers, *you* are the eternal debtor, the rest are the creditors never to be paid off. You must not question their right to your sacrifice, or the nature of their wishes and their needs: their right is conferred upon them by a negative, by the fact that they are 'non-you.'

"For those of you who might ask questions, your code provides a consolation prize and booby-trap: it is for your own happiness, it says, that you must serve the happiness of others, the only way to achieve your joy is to give it up to others, the only way to achieve your prosperity is to surrender your wealth to others, the only way to protect your life is to protect all men except yourself—and if you find no joy in this procedure, it is your own fault and the proof of your evil; if you were good, you would find your happiness in providing a banquet for others, and your dignity in existing on such crumbs as *they* might care to toss you.

"You who have no standard of self-esteem, accept the guilt and dare not ask the questions. But you know the un-admitted answer, refusing to acknowledge what you see, what hidden premise moves your world. You know it, not in honest statement, but as a dark uneasiness within you, while you flounder between guiltily cheating and grudgingly practicing a principle too vicious to name.

"I, who do not accept the unearned, neither in values nor in *guilt*, am here to ask the questions you evaded. Why is it moral to serve the happiness of others, but not your own? If enjoyment is a value, why is it moral when experienced by others, but immoral when experienced by you? If the sensation of eating a cake is a value, why is it an immoral indulgence in your stomach, but a moral goal for you to achieve in the stomach of others? Why is it immoral for you to desire, but moral for others to do so? Why is it immoral to produce a value and keep it, but moral to give it away? And if it is not moral for you to keep a value, why is it moral for others to accept it? If you are selfless and virtuous when you give it, are they not selfish and vicious when they take it? Does virtue consist of serving vice? Is the moral purpose of those who are good, self-immolation for the sake of those who are evil?

"The answer you evade, the monstrous answer is: No, the takers are not evil, provided they did not *earn* the value you gave them. It is not immoral for them to accept it, provided they are unable to produce it, unable to deserve it, unable to give you any value in return. It is not immoral for them to enjoy it, provided they do not obtain it *by right*.

"Such is the secret core of your creed, the other half of your double standard: it is immoral to live by your own effort, but moral to live by the effort of others—it is immoral to consume your own product, but moral to consume the products of others—it is immoral to earn, but moral to mooch—it is the parasites who are the moral justification for the existence of the producers, but the existence of the parasites is an end in itself—it is evil to profit by achievement, but good to profit by sacrifice—it is evil to create your own happiness, but good to enjoy it at the price of the blood of others.

"Your code divides mankind into two castes and commands them to live by opposite rules: those who may desire anything and those who may desire nothing, the chosen and the damned, the riders and the carriers, the eaters and the eaten. What standard determines your caste? What passkey admits you to the moral elite? The passkey is *lack of value*.

"Whatever the value involved, it is your lack of it that gives you a claim upon those who don't lack it. It is your *need* that gives you a claim to rewards. If you are able to satisfy your need, your ability annuls your right to satisfy it. But a need you are *unable* to satisfy gives you first right to the lives of mankind.

"If you succeed, any man who fails is your master; if you fail, any man who succeeds is your serf. Whether your failure is just or not, whether your wishes are rational or not, whether your misfortune is undeserved or the result of your vices, it is *misfortune* that gives you a right to rewards. It is *pain*, regardless of its nature or cause, pain as a primary absolute, that gives you a mortgage on all of existence.

"If you heal your pain by your own effort, you receive no moral credit: your code regards it scornfully as an act of self-interest. Whatever value you seek to acquire, be it wealth or food or love or rights, if you acquire it by means of your virtue, your code does not regard it as a moral acquisition: you occasion no loss to anyone, it is a trade, not alms; a payment, not a sacrifice. The *deserved* belongs in the selfish, commercial realm of mutual profit; it is only the *undeserved* that calls for that moral transaction which consists of profit to one at the price of disaster to the other. To demand rewards for your virtue is selfish and immoral; it is your *lack of virtue* that transforms your demand into a moral right.

"A morality that holds *need* as a claim, holds emptiness—non-existence—as its standard of value; it rewards an *absence*, a defect: weakness, inability, incompetence, suffering, disease, disaster, the lack, the fault, the flaw—the *zero*.

"Who provides the account to pay these claims? Those who are cursed for being non-zeros, each to the extent of his distance from that ideal. Since all values are the product of virtues, the degree of your virtue is used as the measure of your penalty; the degree of your faults is used as the measure of your gain. Your code declares that the rational man must sacrifice himself to the irrational, the independent man to parasites, the honest man to the dishonest, the man of justice to the unjust, the productive man to thieving loafers, the man of integrity to compromising knaves, the man of self-esteem to sniveling neurotics. Do you wonder at the meanness of soul in those you see around you? The man who achieves these virtues will not accept your moral code; the man who accepts your moral code will not achieve these virtues.

"Under a morality of sacrifice, the first value you sacrifice is morality; the next is self-esteem. When need is the standard, every man is both victim and parasite. As a victim, he must labor to fill the needs of others, leaving himself in the position of a parasite whose needs must be filled by others. He cannot approach his fellow men except in one of two disgraceful roles: he is both a beggar and a sucker.

"You fear the man who has a dollar less than you, that dollar is rightfully his, he makes you feel like a moral defrauder. You hate the man who has a dollar more than you, that dollar is rightfully yours, he makes you feel that you are morally defrauded. The man below is a source of your guilt, the man above is a source of your frustration. You do not know what to surrender or demand, when to give and when to grab, what pleasure in life is rightfully yours and what debt is still unpaid to others—you struggle to evade, as 'theory,' the knowledge that by the moral standard you've accepted you are guilty every moment of your life, there is no mouthful of food you swallow that is not *needed* by someone somewhere on earth—and you give up the problem in blind resentment, you conclude that moral perfection is not to be achieved *or desired,* that you will muddle through by snatching as snatch can and by avoiding the eyes of the young, of those who look at you as if self-esteem were possible and they expected you to have it. Guilt is all that you retain within your soul—and so does every other man, as he goes past, avoiding *your* eyes. Do you wonder why your morality has not achieved brotherhood on earth or the good will of man to man?

"The justification of sacrifice, that your morality propounds, is more corrupt than the corruption it purports to justify. The motive of your sacrifice, it tells you, should be *love*—the love you ought to feel for every man. A morality that professes the belief that the values of the spirit are more precious than matter, a morality that teaches you to scorn

a whore who gives her body indiscriminately to all men—
this same morality demands that you surrender your soul
to promiscuous love for all comers.

"As there can be no causeless wealth, so there can be no
causeless love or any sort of causeless emotion. An emotion
is a response to a fact of reality, an estimate dictated by
your standards. To love is to *value*. The man who tells you
that it is possible to value without values, to love those whom
you appraise as worthless, is the man who tells you that it
is possible to grow rich by consuming without producing and
that paper money is as valuable as gold.

"Observe that he does not expect you to feel a causeless
fear. When his kind get into power, they are expert at con-
triving means of terror, at giving you ample cause to feel the
fear by which they desire to rule you. But when it comes to
love, the highest of emotions, you permit them to shriek at
you accusingly that you are a moral delinquent if you're
incapable of feeling causeless love. When a man feels fear
without reason, you call him to the attention of a psychiatrist;
you are not so careful to protect the meaning, the nature
and the dignity of love.

"Love is the expression of one's values, the greatest reward you can earn for the moral qualities you have achieved
in your character and person, the emotional price paid
by one man for the joy he receives from the virtues of another. Your morality demands that you divorce your love
from values and hand it down to any vagrant, not as response
to his worth, but as response to his *need*, not as reward, but
as alms, not as a payment for virtues, but as a blank check
on vices. Your morality tells you that the purpose of love is
to set you free of the bonds of morality, that love is superior
to moral judgment, that true love transcends, forgives and
survives every manner of evil in its object, and the greater
the love the greater the depravity it permits to the loved.
To love a man for his virtues is paltry and human, it tells
you; to love him for his flaws is divine. To love those who
are worthy of it is self-interest; to love the unworthy is
sacrifice. You owe your love to those who don't deserve it,
and the less they deserve it, the more love you owe them—
the more loathsome the object, the nobler your love—the
more unfastidious your love, the greater your virtue—and
if you can bring your soul to the state of a dump heap that
welcomes anything on equal terms, if you can cease to value

moral values, you have achieved the state of moral perfection.

"Such is your morality of sacrifice and such are the twin ideals it offers: to refashion the life of your body in the image of a human stockyard, and the life of your spirit in the image of a dump.

"Such was your goal—and you've reached it. Why do you now moan complaints about man's impotence and the futility of human aspirations? Because you were unable to prosper by seeking destruction? Because you were unable to find joy by worshipping pain? Because you were unable to live by holding death as your standard of value?

"The degree of your ability to live was the degree to which you broke your moral code, yet you believe that those who preach it are friends of humanity, you damn yourself and dare not question their motives or their goals. Take a look at them now, when you face your last choice—and if you choose to perish, do so with full knowledge of how cheaply how small an enemy has claimed your life.

"The mystics of both schools, who preach the creed of sacrifice, are germs that attack you through a single sore: your fear of relying on your mind. They tell you that they possess a means of knowledge higher than the mind, a mode of consciousness superior to reason—like a special pull with some bureaucrat of the universe who gives them secret tips withheld from others. The mystics of spirit declare that they possess an extra sense you lack: this special sixth sense consists of contradicting the whole of the knowledge of your five. The mystics of muscle do not bother to assert any claim to extrasensory perception: they merely declare that your senses are not valid, and that their wisdom consists of perceiving your blindness by some manner of unspecified means. Both kinds demand that you invalidate your own consciousness and surrender yourself into their power. They offer you, as proof of their superior knowledge, the fact that they assert the opposite of everything you know, and as proof of their superior ability to deal with existence, the fact that they lead you to misery, self-sacrifice, starvation, destruction.

"They claim that they perceive a mode of being superior to your existence on this earth. The mystics of spirit call it 'another dimension,' which consists of denying dimensions. The mystics of muscle call it 'the future,' which consists of denying the present. To exist is to possess identity. What identity are they able to give to their superior realm? They keep telling you what it is *not*, but never tell you what it *is*. All their identifications consist of negating: God is that which no human mind can know, they say—and proceed to demand that you consider it knowledge—God is non-man, heaven is non-earth, soul is non-body, virtue is non-profit, A is non-A, perception is non-sensory, knowledge is non-reason. Their definitions are not acts of defining, but of wiping out.

"It is only the metaphysics of a leech that would cling to the idea of a universe where a zero is a standard of identification. A leech would want to seek escape from the necessity to name its own nature—escape from the necessity to know that the substance on which it builds its private universe is blood.

"What is the nature of that superior world to which they sacrifice the world that exists? The mystics of spirit curse matter, the mystics of muscle curse profit. The first wish men to profit by renouncing the earth, the second wish men to inherit the earth by renouncing all profit. Their non-material, non-profit worlds are realms where rivers run with milk and coffee, where wine spurts from rocks at their command, where pastry drops on them from clouds at the price of opening their mouth. On this material, profit-chasing earth, an enormous investment of virtue—of intelligence, integrity, energy, skill—is required to construct a railroad to carry them the distance of one mile; in their non-material, non-profit world, they travel from planet to planet at the cost of a wish. If an honest person asks them: 'How?'—they answer with righteous scorn that a 'how' is the concept of vulgar realists; the concept of superior spirits is 'Somehow.' On this earth restricted by matter and profit, rewards are achieved by thought; in a world set free of such restrictions rewards are achieved by wishing.

"And *that* is the whole of their shabby secret. The secret of all their esoteric philosophies, of all their dialectics and super-senses, of their evasive eyes and snarling words, the secret for which they destroy civilization, language, industries and lives, the secret for which they pierce their own eyes and eardrums, grind out their senses, blank out their minds, the purpose for which they dissolve the absolutes of reason, logic, matter, existence, reality—is to erect upon that plastic fog a single holy absolute: their *Wish*.

"The restriction they seek to escape is the law of identity. The freedom they seek is freedom from the fact that an A will remain an A, no matter what their tears or tantrums— that a river will not bring them milk, no matter what their hunger—that water will not run uphill, no matter what comforts they could gain if it did, and if they want to lift it to the roof of a skyscraper, they must do it by a process of thought and labor, in which the nature of an inch of pipeline counts, but their feelings do not—that their feelings are impotent to alter the course of a single speck of dust in space or the nature of any action they have committed.

"Those who tell you that man is unable to perceive a reality undistorted by his senses, mean that they are unwilling to perceive a reality undistorted by their feelings. 'Things as they are' are things as perceived by your mind; divorce them from reason and they become 'things as perceived by your wishes.'

"There is no honest revolt against reason—and when you accept any part of their creed, your motive is to get away with something your reason would not permit you to attempt. The freedom you seek is freedom from the fact that if you stole your wealth, you are a scoundrel, no matter how much you give to charity or how many prayers you recite—that if you sleep with sluts, you're not a worthy husband, no matter how anxiously you feel that you love your wife next morning—that you are an entity, not a series of random pieces scattered through a universe where nothing sticks and nothing commits you to anything, the universe of a child's nightmare where identities switch and swim, where the rotter and the hero are interchangeable parts arbitrarily assumed at will—that you are a man—that you are an entity—that you *are*.

"No matter how eagerly you claim that the goal of your mystic wishing is a higher mode of life, the rebellion against identity is the wish for non-existence. The desire not to be anything is the desire not to be.

"Your teachers, the mystics of both schools, have reversed causality in their consciousness, then strive to reverse it in existence. They take their emotions as a cause, and their mind as a passive effect. They make their emotions their tool for perceiving reality. They hold their desires as an irreducible primary, as a fact superseding all facts. An honest man does not desire until he has identified the object of his desire. He says: 'It is, therefore I want it.' They say: 'I want it, therefore it is.'

"They want to cheat the axiom of existence and consciousness, they want their consciousness to be an instrument not of *perceiving* but of *creating* existence, and existence to be not the *object* but the *subject* of their consciousness—they want to be that God they created in their image and likeness, who creates a universe out of a void by means of an arbitrary whim. But reality is not to be cheated. What they achieve is the opposite of their desire. They want an omnipotent power over existence; instead, they lose the power of their consciousness. By refusing to know, they condemn themselves to the horror of a perpetual unknown.

"Those irrational wishes that draw you to their creed, those emotions you worship as an idol, on whose altar you sacrifice the earth, that dark, incoherent passion within you, which you take as the voice of God or of your glands, is nothing more than the corpse of your mind. An emotion that clashes with your reason, an emotion that you cannot explain or control, is only the carcass of that stale thinking which you forbade your mind to revise.

"Whenever you committed the evil of refusing to think and to see, of exempting from the absolute of reality some one small wish of yours, whenever you chose to say: Let me withdraw from the judgment of reason the cookies I stole, or the existence of God, let me have my one irrational whim and I will be a man of reason about all else —*that* was the act of subverting your consciousness, the act of corrupting your mind. Your mind then became a fixed jury who takes orders from a secret underworld, whose verdict distorts the evidence to fit an absolute it dares not touch—and a censored reality is the result, a splintered reality where the bits you chose to see are floating among the chasms of those you didn't, held together by that embalming fluid of the mind which is an emotion exempted from thought.

"The links you strive to drown are causal connections. The enemy you seek to defeat is the law of causality: it permits you no miracles. The law of causality is the law of identity applied to action. All actions are caused by entities. The nature of an action is caused and determined by the nature of the entities that act; a thing cannot act in contradiction to its nature. An action not caused by an entity would be caused by a zero, which would mean a *zero* controlling a *thing*, a non-entity controlling an entity, the non-existent ruling the existent—which is the universe of your teachers' desire, the *cause* of their doctrines of causeless action, the *reason* of their revolt against reason, the goal of their morality, their politics, their economics, the ideal they strive for: the reign of the zero.

"The law of identity does not permit you to have your cake and eat it, too. The law of causality does not permit you to eat your cake *before* you have it. But if you drown both laws in the blanks of your mind, if you pretend to yourself and to others that you don't see—then you can try to proclaim your right to eat your cake today and mine tomorrow, you can preach that the way to have a cake is to eat it first, before you bake it, that the way to produce is to start by consuming, that all wishers have an equal claim to all things, since nothing is caused by anything. The corollary of the *causeless* in matter is the *unearned* in spirit.

"Whenever you rebel against causality, your motive is the fraudulent desire, not to escape it, but worse: to reverse it. You want unearned love, as if love, the effect, could give you personal value, the cause—you want unearned admiration, as if admiration, the effect, could give you virtue, the cause—you want unearned wealth, as if wealth, the effect, could give you ability, the cause—you plead for mercy, *mercy*, not justice, as if an unearned forgiveness could wipe out the *cause* of your plea. And to indulge your ugly little shams, you support the doctrines of your teachers, while they run hog-wild proclaiming that spending, the effect, creates riches, the cause, that machinery, the effect, creates intelligence, the cause, that your sexual desires, the effect, create your philosophical values, the cause.

"Who pays for the orgy? Who causes the causeless? Who are the victims, condemned to remain unacknowledged and to perish in silence, lest their agony disturb your pretense that they do not exist? *We* are, we, the men of the mind.

"We are the *cause* of all the values that you covet, we who perform the process of *thinking*, which is the process of defining *identity* and discovering *causal connections*. We taught you to know, to speak, to produce, to desire, to love. You who abandon reason—were it not for us who preserve it, you would not be able to fulfil or even to conceive your wishes. You would not be able to desire the clothes that had not been made, the automobile that had not been invented, the money that had not been devised, as exchange for goods that did not exist, the admiration that had not been experienced for men who had achieved nothing, the love that belongs and pertains only to those who preserve their capacity to think, to choose, *to value*.

"You—who leap like a savage out of the jungle of your feelings into the Fifth Avenue of *our* New York and proclaim that you want to keep the electric lights, but to destroy the generators—it is *our* wealth that you use while destroying us, it is *our* values that you use while damning us, it is *our* language that you use while denying the mind.

"Just as your mystics of spirit invented their heaven in the image of our earth, omitting our existence, and promised you rewards created by miracle out of non-matter—so your modern mystics of muscle omit our existence and promise you a heaven where matter shapes itself of its own causeless will into all the rewards desired by your non-mind.

"For centuries, the mystics of spirit had existed by running a protection racket—by making life on earth unbearable, then charging you for consolation and relief, by forbidding all the virtues that make existence possible, then riding on the shoulders of your guilt, by declaring production and joy to be sins, then collecting blackmail from the sinners. We, the men of the mind, were the unnamed victims of their creed, we who were willing to break their moral code and to bear damnation for the sin of reason—we who thought and acted, while they wished and prayed—we who were moral outcasts, we who were bootleggers of life when life was held to be a crime—while they basked in moral glory for the virtue of surpassing material greed and of distributing in selfless charity the material goods produced by—blank-out.

"*Now* we are chained and commanded to produce by savages who do not grant us even the identification of sinners —by savages who proclaim that we do not exist, then threaten to deprive us of the life we don't possess, if we fail to provide them with the goods we don't produce. Now we are expected to continue running railroads and to know the minute when a train will arrive after crossing the span of a continent; we are expected to continue running steel mills and to know the molecular structure of every drop of metal

in the cables of your bridges and in the body of the airplanes that support you in mid-air—while the tribes of your
grotesque little mystics of muscle fight over the carcass of
our world, gibbering in sounds of non-language that there
are no principles, no absolutes, no knowledge, no mind.

"Dropping below the level of a savage, who believes that
the magic words he utters have the power to alter reality,
they believe that reality can be altered by the power of the
words they do *not* utter—and their magic tool is the blank-
out, the pretense that nothing can come into existence past
the voodoo of their refusal to identify it.

"As they feed on stolen wealth in body, so they feed on
stolen concepts in mind, and proclaim that honesty consists
of refusing to know that one is stealing. As they use effects
while denying causes, so they use our concepts while denying
the roots and the existence of the concepts they are using.
As they seek, not to build, but to *take over* industrial plants,
so they seek, not to think, but to *take over* human thinking.

"As they proclaim that the only requirement for running a
factory is the ability to turn the cranks of the machines, and
blank out the question of who created the factory—so they
proclaim that there are no entities, that nothing exists but
motion, and blank out the fact that *motion* presupposes the
thing which moves, that without the concept of entity, there
can be no such concept as 'motion.' As they proclaim their
right to consume the unearned, and blank out the question
of who's to produce it—so they proclaim that there is no
law of identity, that nothing exists but change, and blank
out the fact that *change* presupposes the concepts of what
changes, from what and to what, that without the law of
identity no such concept as 'change' is possible. As they rob
an industrialist while denying his value, so they seek to
seize power over all of existence while denying that existence exists.

" 'We know that we know nothing,' they chatter, blanking
out the fact that they are claiming knowledge—'There are no
absolutes,' they chatter, blanking out the fact that they are
uttering an absolute—'You cannot *prove* that you exist or
that you're conscious,' they chatter, blanking out the fact
that *proof* presupposes existence, consciousness and a complex chain of knowledge: the existence of something to know,
of a consciousness able to know it, and of a knowledge that

has learned to distinguish between such concepts as the proved and the unproved.

"When a savage who has not learned to speak declares that existence must be proved, he is asking you to prove it by means of non-existence—when he declares that your consciousness must be proved, he is asking you to prove it by means of unconsciousness—he is asking you to step into a void outside of existence and consciousness to give him proof of both—he is asking you to become a zero gaining knowledge about a zero.

"When he declares that an axiom is a matter of arbitrary choice and he doesn't choose to accept the axiom that he exists, he blanks out the fact that he has accepted it by uttering that sentence, that the only way to reject it is to shut one's mouth, expound no theories and die.

"An axiom is a statement that identifies the base of knowledge and of any further statement pertaining to that knowledge, a statement necessarily contained in all others, whether any particular speaker chooses to identify it or not. An axiom is a proposition that defeats its opponents by the fact that they have to accept it and use it in the process of any attempt to deny it. Let the caveman who does not choose to accept the axiom of identity, try to present his theory without using the concept of identity or any concept derived from it —let the anthropoid who does not choose to accept the existence of nouns, try to devise a language without nouns, adjectives or verbs—let the witch doctor who does not choose to accept the validity of sensory perception, try to prove it without using the data he obtained by sensory perception—let the head-hunter who does not choose to accept the validity of logic, try to prove it without using logic—let the pigmy who proclaims that a skyscraper needs no foundation after it reaches its fiftieth story, yank the base from under *his* building, not yours—let the cannibal who snarls that the freedom of man's mind was needed to *create* an industrial civilization, but is not needed to *maintain* it, be given an arrowhead and bearskin, not a university chair of economics.

"Do you think they are taking you back to dark ages? They are taking you back to darker ages than any your history has known. Their goal is not the era of pre-science, but the era of pre-language. Their purpose is to deprive you of the concept on which man's mind, his life and his culture depend: the concept of an *objective* reality. Identify the development of a human consciousness—and you will know the purpose of their creed.

"A savage is a being who has not grasped that A is A and that reality is real. He has arrested his mind at the level of a baby's, at the stage when a consciousness acquires its initial sensory perceptions and has not learned to distinguish solid objects. It is to a baby that the world appears as a blur of motion, without things that move—and the birth of his mind is the day when he grasps that the streak that keeps flickering past him is his mother and the whirl beyond her is a curtain, that the two are solid entities and neither can turn into the other, that they *are* what they are, that they *exist*. The day when he grasps that matter has no volition is the day when he grasps that *he* has—and this is his birth as a *human* being. The day when he grasps that the reflection he sees in a mirror is not a delusion, that it is real, but it is not himself, that the mirage he sees in a desert is not a delusion, that the air and the light rays that cause it are real, but it is not a city, it is a city's reflection—the day when he grasps that he is not a passive recipient of the sensations of any given moment, that his senses do not provide him with automatic knowledge in separate snatches independent of context, but only with the material of knowledge, which his mind must learn to integrate—the day when he grasps that his senses cannot deceive him, that physical objects cannot act without causes, that his organs of perception are physical and have no volition, no power to invent or to distort, that the evidence they give him is an absolute, but his mind must learn to understand it, his mind must discover the nature, the causes, the full context of his sensory material, his mind must identify the things that he perceives—*that* is the day of his birth as a thinker and scientist.

"*We* are the men who reach that day; you are the men who choose to reach it partly; a savage is a man who never does.

"To a savage, the world is a place of unintelligible miracles where anything is possible to inanimate matter and nothing is possible to *him*. His world is not the unknown, but that irrational horror: the unknowable. He believes that physical objects are endowed with a mysterious volition, moved by *causeless*, unpredictable whims, while *he* is a helpless pawn at the mercy of forces beyond his control. He believes that nature is ruled by demons who possess an omnipotent power and that reality is their fluid plaything, where they can turn his bowl of meal into a snake and his wife into a beetle at any moment, where the A he has never discovered can be any non-A they choose, where the only knowledge he possesses is that he must not attempt to know. He can count on nothing, he can only *wish*, and he spends his life on wishing, on begging his demons to grant him his wishes by the arbitrary power of their will, giving them credit when they do, taking the blame when they don't, offering them sacrifices in token of his gratitude and sacrifices in token of his guilt, crawling on his belly in fear and worship of sun and moon and wind and rain and of any thug who announces himself as their spokesman, provided his words are unintelligible and his mask sufficiently frightening—he wishes, begs and crawls, and dies, leaving you, as a record of his view of existence, the distorted monstrosities of his idols, part-man, part-animal, part-spider, the embodiments of the world of non-A.

"*His* is the intellectual state of your modern teachers and *his* is the world to which they want to bring you.

"If you wonder by what means they propose to do it, walk into any college classroom and you will hear your professors teaching your children that man can be certain of nothing, that his consciousness has no validity whatever, that he can learn no facts and no laws of existence, that he's incapable of knowing an objective reality. What, then, is his standard of knowledge and truth? Whatever others *believe*, is their answer. There is no knowledge, they teach, there's only *faith:* your belief that you exist is an act of faith, no more valid than another's faith in his right to kill you; the axioms of science are an act of faith, no more valid than a mystic's faith in revelations; the belief that electric light can be produced by a generator is an act of faith, no more valid than the belief that it can be produced by a rabbit's foot kissed under a stepladder on the first of the moon—truth is whatever people want it to be, and *people* are everyone except yourself; reality is whatever people choose to say it is, there are no objective facts, there are only people's arbitrary wishes—a man who seeks knowledge in a laboratory by means of test tubes and logic is an old-fashioned, superstitious fool; a true scientist is a man who goes around taking public polls—and if it weren't for the selfish greed of the manufacturers of steel girders, who have a vested interest in obstructing the progress of science, you would learn that New York City does not exist, because a poll of the entire population of the world would tell you by a landslide majority that their *beliefs* forbid its existence.

"For centuries, the mystics of spirit have proclaimed that faith is superior to reason, but have not dared deny the existence of reason. Their heirs and product, the mystics of muscle, have completed their job and achieved their dream: they proclaim that everything is faith, and call it a revolt against believing. As revolt against unproved assertions, they proclaim that nothing can be proved; as revolt against supernatural knowledge, they proclaim that no knowledge is possible; as revolt against the enemies of science, they proclaim that science is superstition; as revolt against the enslavement of the mind, they proclaim that there is no mind.

"If you surrender your power to perceive, if you accept the switch of your standard from the *objective* to the *collective* and wait for mankind to tell you what to think, you will find another switch taking place before the eyes you have renounced: you will find that your teachers become the rulers of the collective, and if you then refuse to obey them, protesting that they are not the whole of mankind, they will answer: 'By what means do you know that we are not? *Are*, brother? Where did you get that old-fashioned term?'

"If you doubt that such is their purpose, observe with what passionate consistency the mystics of muscle are striving to make you forget that a concept such as '*mind*' has ever existed. Observe the twists of undefined verbiage, the words with rubber meanings, the terms left floating in midstream, by means of which they try to get around the recognition of the concept of '*thinking*.' Your consciousness, they tell you, consists of 'reflexes,' 'reactions,' 'experiences,' 'urges,' and 'drives'—and refuse to identify the means by which they acquired that knowledge, to identify the act they are performing when they tell it or the act you are performing when you listen. Words have the power to 'condition' you, they say and refuse to identify the reason why words have the power to change your—blank-out. A student reading a book understands it through a process of—blank-out. A scientist working on an invention is engaged in the activity of—blank-out. A psychologist helping a neurotic to solve a problem and untangle a conflict, does it by means of—blank-out. An industrialist—blank-out—there is no such person. A factory is a 'natural resource,' like a tree, a rock or a mud puddle.

"The problem of production, they tell you, has been solved and deserves no study or concern; the only problem left for your 'reflexes' to solve is now the problem of distribution. Who solved the problem of production? Humanity, they answer. What was the solution? The goods are here. How did they get here? Somehow. What caused it? Nothing has causes.

"They proclaim that every man born is entitled to exist without labor and, the laws of reality to the contrary notwithstanding, is entitled to receive his 'minimum sustenance' —his food, his clothes, his shelter—with no effort on his part, as his due and his birthright. To receive it—from whom? Blank-out. Every man, they announce, owns an equal share of the technological benefits created in the world. Created— by whom? Blank-out. Frantic cowards who posture as defenders of industrialists now define the purpose of economics as 'an adjustment between the unlimited *desires* of men and the goods supplied in limited quantity.' Supplied—by whom? Blank-out. Intellectual hoodlums who pose as professors, shrug away the thinkers of the past by declaring that their social theories were based on the impractical assumption that man was a rational being—but since men are not rational, they declare, there ought to be established a system that will make it possible for them to exist while being *irrational*, which means: while defying reality. Who will make it possible? Blank-out. Any stray mediocrity rushes into print with plans to control the production of mankind—and whoever agrees or disagrees with his statistics, no one questions his right to enforce his plans by means of a gun. Enforce—on whom? Blank-out. Random females with causeless incomes flitter on trips around the globe and return to deliver the message that the backward peoples of the world *demand* a higher standard of living. Demand—of whom? Blank-out.

"And to forestall any inquiry into the cause of the difference between a jungle village and New York City, they resort to the ultimate obscenity of explaining man's industrial progress—skyscrapers, cable bridges, power motors, railroad trains—by declaring that man is an animal who possesses an *'instinct of tool-making.'*

"Did you wonder what is wrong with the world? You are now seeing the climax of the creed of the uncaused and unearned. All your gangs of mystics, of spirit or muscle, are fighting one another for power to rule you, snarling that love is the solution for all the problems of your spirit and that a whip is the solution for all the problems of your body—you who have agreed to have no mind. Granting man less dignity than they grant to cattle, ignoring what an animal trainer could tell them—that no animal can be trained by fear, that a tortured elephant will trample its torturer, but will not work for him or carry his burdens—they expect man to continue to produce electronic tubes, supersonic airplanes, atom-smashing engines and interstellar telescopes, with his ration of meat for reward and a lash on his back for incentive.

"Make no mistake about the character of mystics. To undercut your consciousness has always been their only purpose throughout the ages—and *power*, the power to rule you by force, has always been their only lust.

"From the rites of the jungle witch doctors, which distorted reality into grotesque absurdities, stunted the minds of their victims and kept them in terror of the supernatural for stagnant stretches of centuries—to the supernatural doctrines of the Middle Ages, which kept men huddling on the mud floors of their hovels, in terror that the devil might steal the soup they had worked eighteen hours to earn—to the seedy little smiling professor who assures you that your brain has no capacity to think, that you have no means of perception and must blindly obey the omnipotent will of that supernatural force: Society—all of it is the same performance for the same and only purpose: to reduce you to the kind of pulp that has surrendered the validity of its consciousness.

"But it cannot be done to you without your consent. If you permit it to be done, you deserve it.

"When you listen to a mystic's harangue on the impotence of the human mind and begin to doubt *your* consciousness, not his, when you permit your precariously semi-rational state to be shaken by any assertion and decide it is safer to trust his superior certainty and knowledge, the joke is on both of you: your sanction is the only source of certainty he has. The supernatural power that a mystic dreads, the unknowable spirit he worships, the consciousness he considers omnipotent is—*yours.*

"A mystic is a man who surrendered his mind at its first encounter with the minds of others. Somewhere in the distant reaches of his childhood, when his own understanding of reality clashed with the assertions of others, with their arbitrary orders and contradictory demands, he gave in to so craven a fear of independence that he renounced his rational faculty. At the crossroads of the choice between 'I know' and 'They say,' he chose the authority of others, he chose to submit rather than to understand, to *believe* rather than to think. Faith in the supernatural begins as faith in the superiority of others. His surrender took the form of the feeling that he must hide his lack of understanding, that others possess some mysterious knowledge of which he alone is deprived, that reality is whatever they want it to be, through some means forever denied to him.

"From then on, afraid to think, he is left at the mercy of unidentified feelings. His feelings become his only guide, his only remnant of personal identity, he clings to them with ferocious possessiveness—and whatever thinking he does is devoted to the struggle of hiding from himself that the nature of his feelings is terror.

"When a mystic declares that he *feels* the existence of a power superior to reason, he feels it all right, but that power is not an omniscient super-spirit of the universe, it is the consciousness of any passer-by to whom he has surrendered his own. A mystic is driven by the urge to impress, to cheat, to flatter, to deceive, *to force* that omnipotent consciousness of others. 'They' are his only key to reality, he feels that he cannot exist save by harnessing their mysterious power and extorting their unaccountable consent. 'They' are his only means of perception and, like a blind man who depends on the sight of a dog, he feels he must leash them in order to live. To control the consciousness of others becomes his only passion; power-lust is a weed that grows only in the vacant lots of an abandoned mind.

"Every dictator is a mystic, and every mystic is a potential dictator. A mystic craves obedience from men, not their agreement. He wants them to surrender their consciousness to his assertions, his edicts, his wishes, his whims—as *his* consciousness is surrendered to theirs. He wants to deal with men by means of faith and force—he finds no satisfaction in their consent if he must earn it by means of facts and reason. Reason is the enemy he dreads and, simultaneously, considers precarious; reason, to him, is a means of deception; he *feels* that men possess some power more potent than reason

—and only their causeless belief or their forced obedience can give him a sense of security, a proof that he has gained control of the mystic endowment he lacked. His lust is to command, not to convince: conviction requires an act of independence and rests on the absolute of an objective reality. What he seeks is power over reality and over men's means of perceiving it, their mind, the power to interpose his will between existence and consciousness, as if, by agreeing to fake the reality he orders them to fake, men would, in fact, create it.

"Just as the mystic is a parasite in matter, who expropriates the wealth created by others—just as he is a parasite in spirit, who plunders the ideas created by others—so he falls below the level of a lunatic who creates his own distortion of reality, to the level of a parasite of lunacy who seeks a distortion created by others.

"There is only one state that fulfills the mystic's longing for infinity, non-causality, non-identity: *death*. No matter what unintelligible causes he ascribes to his incommunicable feelings, whoever rejects reality rejects existence—and the feelings that move him from then on are hatred for all the values of man's life, and lust for all the evils that destroy it. A mystic relishes the spectacle of suffering, of poverty, subservience and terror; these give him a feeling of triumph, a proof of the defeat of rational reality. But no other reality exists.

"No matter whose welfare he professes to serve, be it the welfare of God or of that disembodied gargoyle he describes as 'The People,' no matter what ideal he proclaims in terms of some supernatural dimension—*in fact, in reality, on earth*, his ideal is *death*, his craving is to kill, his only satisfaction is to torture.

"Destruction is the only end that the mystics' creed has ever achieved as it is the only end that you see them achieving today, and if the ravages wrought by their acts have not made them question their doctrines, if they profess to be moved by love, yet are not deterred by piles of human corpses, it is because the truth about their souls is worse than the obscene excuse you have allowed them, the excuse that the end justifies the means and that the horrors they practice are means to nobler ends. The truth is that those horrors are their ends.

"You who're depraved enough to believe that you could

adjust yourself to a mystic's dictatorship and could please him by obeying his orders—there is no way to please him; when you obey, he will reverse his orders; he seeks obedience for the sake of obedience and destruction for the sake of destruction. You who are craven enough to believe that you can make terms with a mystic by giving in to his extortions —there is no way to buy him off, the bribe he wants is your life, as slowly or as fast as you are willing to give it in —and the monster he seeks to bribe is the hidden blank-out in his mind, which drives him to kill in order not to learn that the death he desires is his own.

"You who are innocent enough to believe that the forces let loose in your world today are moved by greed for material plunder—the mystics' scramble for spoils is only a screen to conceal from their mind the nature of their motive. Wealth is a means of human life, and they clamor for wealth in imitation of living beings, to pretend to themselves that they desire to live. But their swinish indulgence in plundered luxury is not enjoyment, it is escape. They do not want to own your fortune, they want you to lose it; they do not want to succeed, they want you to fail; they do not want to live, they want you to die; they desire nothing, they hate existence, and they keep running, each trying not to learn that the object of his hatred is himself.

"You who've never grasped the nature of evil, you who describe them as 'misguided idealists'—may the God you invented forgive you!—*they* are the essence of evil, they, those anti-living objects who seek, by devouring the world, to fill the *selfless* zero of their soul. It is not your wealth that they're after. Theirs is a conspiracy against the mind, which means: against life and man.

"It is a conspiracy without leader or direction, and the random little thugs of the moment who cash in on the agony of one land or another are chance scum riding the torrent from the broken dam of the sewer of centuries, from the reservoir of hatred for reason, for logic, for ability, for achievement, for joy, stored by every whining anti-human who ever preached the superiority of the 'heart' over the mind.

"It is a conspiracy of all those who seek, not to live, but to *get away with living*, those who seek to cut just one small corner of reality and are drawn, by feeling, to all the others who are busy cutting other corners—a conspiracy that unites by links of evasion all those who pursue a *zero* as a value: the professor who, unable to think, takes pleasure in crippling the mind of his students, the businessman who, to protect his stagnation, takes pleasure in chaining the ability of competitors, the neurotic who, to defend his self-loathing, takes pleasure in breaking men of self-esteem, the incompetent who takes pleasure in defeating achievement, the mediocrity who takes pleasure in demolishing greatness, the eunuch who takes pleasure in the castration of all pleasure—and all their intellectual munition-makers, all those who preach that the immolation of virtue will transform vices into virtue. *Death* is the premise at the root of their theories, *death* is the goal of their actions in practice—and *you* are the last of their victims.

"We, who were the living buffers between you and the nature of your creed, are no longer there to save you from the effects of your chosen beliefs. We are no longer willing to pay with our lives the debts you incurred in yours or the moral deficit piled up by all the generations behind you. You had been living on borrowed time—and I am the man who has called in the loan.

"I am the man whose existence your blank-outs were intended to permit you to ignore. I am the man whom you did not want either to live or to die. You did not want me to live, because you were afraid of knowing that I carried the responsibility you dropped and that your lives depended upon me; you did not want me to die, because you knew it.

"Twelve years ago, when I worked in your world, I was an inventor. I was one of a profession that came last in human history and will be first to vanish on the way back to the sub-human. An inventor is a man who asks 'Why?' of the universe and lets nothing stand between the answer and his mind.

"Like the man who discovered the use of steam or the man who discovered the use of oil, I discovered a source of energy which was available since the birth of the globe, but which men had not known how to use except as an object of worship, of terror and of legends about a thundering god. I completed the experimental model of a motor that would have made a fortune for me and for those who had hired me, a motor that would have raised the efficiency of every human installation using power and would have added the

gift of higher productivity to every hour you spend at earning your living.

"Then, one night at a factory meeting, I heard myself
sentenced to death by reason of my achievement. I heard
three parasites assert that my brain and my life were their
property, that my right to exist was conditional and depended on the satisfaction of their desires. The purpose of my
ability, they said, was to serve the needs of those who were
less able. I had no right to live, they said, by reason of my
competence for living; their right to live was unconditional,
by reason of their incompetence.

"Then I saw what was wrong with the world, I saw what
destroyed men and nations, and where the battle for life
had to be fought. I saw that the enemy was an inverted
morality—and that my sanction was its only power. I saw that
evil was impotent—that evil was the irrational, the blind,
the anti-real—and that the only weapon of its triumph was
the willingness of the good to serve it. Just as the parasites
around me were proclaiming their helpless dependence on
my mind and were expecting me voluntarily to accept a slavery they had no power to enforce, just as they were counting
on my self-immolation to provide them with the means of
their plan—so throughout the world and throughout men's
history, in every version and form, from the extortions of
loafing relatives to the atrocities of collectivized countries, it
is the good, the able, the men of reason, who act as their
own destroyers, who transfuse to evil the blood of their virtue and let evil transmit to them the poison of destruction,
thus gaining for evil the power of survival, and for their
own values—the impotence of death. I saw that there comes
a point, in the defeat of any man of virtue, when his own
consent is needed for evil to win—and that no manner of
injury done to him by others can succeed if he chooses to
withhold his consent. I saw that I could put an end to your
outrages by pronouncing a single word in my mind. I pro-
nounced it. The word was 'No.'

"I quit that factory. I quit your world. I made it my job
to warn your victims and to give them the method and the
weapon to fight you. The method was to refuse to deflect
retribution. The weapon was justice.

"If you want to know what you lost when I quit and when
my strikers deserted your world—stand on an empty stretch

of soil in a wilderness unexplored by men and ask yourself
what manner of survival you would achieve and how long
you would last if you refused to think, with no one around
to teach you the motions, or, if you chose to think, how
much your mind would be able to discover—ask yourself
how many independent conclusions you have reached in the
course of your life and how much of your time was spent
on performing the actions you learned from others—ask
yourself whether you would be able to discover how to
till the soil and grow your food, whether you would be
able to invent a wheel, a lever, an induction coil, a generator,
an electronic tube—then decide whether men of ability
are exploiters who live by the fruit of *your* labor and rob
you of the wealth that *you* produce, and whether you dare
to believe that you possess the power to enslave them.
Let your women take a look at a jungle female with
her shriveled face and pendulous breasts, as she sits grinding
meal in a bowl, hour after hour, century by century—then
let them ask themselves whether their 'instinct of tool-making' will provide them with their electric refrigerators, their
washing machines and vacuum cleaners, and, if not, whether
they care to destroy those who provided it all, but not 'by
instinct.'

"Take a look around you, you savages who stutter that
ideas are created by men's means of production, that a machine is not the product of human thought, but a mystical
power that produces human thinking. You have never discovered the industrial age—and you cling to the morality of
the barbarian eras when a miserable form of human subsistence was produced by the muscular labor of slaves. Every
mystic had always longed for slaves, to protect him from the
material reality he dreaded. But *you*, you grotesque little
atavists, stare blindly at the skyscrapers and smokestacks
around you and dream of enslaving the material providers
who are scientists, inventors, industrialists. When you clamor
for public ownership of the means of production, you are
clamoring for public ownership of the mind. I have taught
my strikers that the answer you deserve is only: 'Try and
get it.'

"You proclaim yourself unable to harness the forces of
inanimate matter, yet propose to harness the minds of men
who are able to achieve the feats you cannot equal. You
proclaim that you cannot survive without us, yet propose to

dictate the terms of our survival. You proclaim that you need us, yet indulge the impertinence of asserting your right to rule us by force—and expect that we, who are not afraid of that physical nature which fills you with terror, will cower at the sight of any lout who has talked you into voting him a chance to command us.

"You propose to establish a social order based on the following tenets: that you're incompetent to run your own life, but competent to run the lives of others—that you're unfit to exist in freedom, but fit to become an omnipotent ruler—that you're unable to earn your living by the use of your own intelligence, but able to judge politicians and to vote them into jobs of total power over arts you have never seen, over sciences you have never studied, over achievements of which you have no knowledge, over the gigantic industries where you, by your own definition of your capacity, would be unable successfully to fill the job of assistant greaser.

"This idol of your cult of zero-worship, this symbol of impotence—the congenital dependent—is your image of man and your standard of value, in whose likeness you strive to refashion your soul. 'It's only human,' you cry in defense of any depravity, reaching the stage of self-abasement where you seek to make the concept 'human' mean the weakling, the fool, the rotter, the liar, the failure, the coward, the fraud, and to exile from the human race the hero, the thinker, the producer, the inventor, the strong, the purposeful, the pure—as if 'to feel' were human, but to think were not, as if to fail were human, but to succeed were not, as if corruption were human, but virtue were not—as if the premise of *death* were proper to man, but the premise of *life* were not.

"In order to deprive us of honor, that you may then deprive us of our wealth, you have always regarded us as slaves who deserve no moral recognition. You praise any venture that claims to be non-profit, and damn the men who made the profits that make the venture possible. You regard as 'in the public interest' any project serving those who do not pay; it is not in the public interest to provide any services for those who do the paying. 'Public benefit' is anything given as alms; to engage in trade is to injure the public. 'Public welfare' is the welfare of those who do not earn it; those who do, are entitled to no welfare. 'The public,' to you, is whoever has failed to achieve any virtue or value; whoever achieves it, whoever provides the goods you require for survival, ceases to be regarded as part of the public or as part of the human race.

"What blank-out permitted you to hope that you could get away with this muck of contradictions and to plan it as an ideal society, when the 'No' of your victims was sufficient to demolish the whole of your structure? What permits any insolent beggar to wave his sores in the face of his betters and to plead for help in the tone of a threat? You cry, as he does, that you are counting on our pity, but your secret hope is the moral code that has taught you to count on our *guilt*. You expect us to feel guilty of our virtues in the presence of your vices, wounds and failures—guilty of succeeding at existence, guilty of enjoying the life that you damn, yet beg us to help you to live.

"Did you want to know who is John Galt? I am the first man of ability who refused to regard it as guilt. I am the first man who would not do penance for my virtues or let them be used as the tools of my destruction. I am the first man who would not suffer martyrdom at the hands of those who wished me to perish for the privilege of keeping them alive. I am the first man who told them that I did not need them, and until they learned to deal with me as traders, giving value for value, they would have to exist without me, as I would exist without them; then I would let them learn whose is the need and whose the ability—and if human survival is the standard, whose terms would set the way to survive.

"I have done by plan and intention what had been done throughout history by silent default. There have always been men of intelligence who went on strike, in protest and despair, but they did not know the meaning of their action. The man who retires from public life, to think, but not to share his thoughts—the man who chooses to spend his years in the obscurity of menial employment, keeping to himself the fire of his mind, never giving it form, expression or reality, refusing to bring it into a world he despises—the man who is defeated by revulsion, the man who renounces before he has started, the man who gives up rather than give in, the man who functions at a fraction of his capacity, disarmed by his longing for an ideal he has not found—they are on strike, on strike against unreason, on strike against your world and your values. But not knowing any values of their own, they abandoned the quest to know—in the darkness of their hopeless indignation, which is righteous without knowledge of the right, and passionate without knowledge of desire, they concede to you the power of reality and surrender the incentives of their mind—and they perish in bitter futility, as rebels who never learned the object of their rebellion, as lovers who never discovered their love.

"The infamous times you call the Dark Ages were an era of intelligence on strike, when men of ability went underground and lived undiscovered, studying in secret, and died, destroying the works of their mind, when only a few of the bravest of martyrs remained to keep the human race alive. Every period ruled by mystics was an era of stagnation and want, when most men were on strike against existence, working for less than their barest survival, leaving nothing but scraps for their rulers to loot, refusing to think, to venture, to produce, when the ultimate collector of their profits and the final authority on truth or error was the whim of some gilded degenerate sanctioned as superior to reason by divine right and by grace of a club. The road of human history was a string of blank-outs over sterile stretches eroded by faith and force, with only a few brief bursts of sunlight, when the released energy of the men of the mind performed the wonders you gaped at, admired and promptly extinguished again.

"But there will be no extinction, this time. The game of the mystics is up. You will perish in and by your own unreality. We, the men of reason, will survive.

"I have called out on strike the kind of martyrs who had never deserted you before. I have given them the weapon they had lacked: the knowledge of their own moral value. I have taught them that the world is ours, whenever we choose to claim it, by virtue and grace of the fact that ours is the Morality of Life. They, the great victims who had produced all the wonders of humanity's brief summer, they, the idustrialists, the conquerors of matter, had not discovered the nature of their right. They had known that theirs was the power. I taught them that theirs was the glory.

"You, who dare to regard us as the moral inferiors of any mystic who claims supernatural visions—you, who scramble like vultures for plundered pennies, yet honor a fortune-teller above a fortune-maker—you, who scorn a businessman as ignoble, but esteem any posturing artist as exalted—the root of your standards is that mystic miasma which comes from primordial swamps, that cult of death, which pronounces a businessman immoral by reason of the fact that he keeps you alive. You, who claim that you long to rise above the crude concerns of the body, above the drudgery of serving mere physical needs—*who* is enslaved by physical needs: the Hindu who labors from sunrise to sunset at the shafts of a hand-plow for a bowl of rice, or the American who is driving a tractor? *Who* is the conqueror of physical reality: the man who sleeps on a bed of nails or the man who sleeps on an inner-spring mattress? *Which* is the monument to the triumph of the human spirit over matter: the germ-eaten hovels on the shorelines of the Ganges or the Atlantic skyline of New York?

"Unless you learn the answers to these questions—and learn to stand at reverent attention when you face the achievements of man's mind—you will not stay much longer on this earth, which we love and will not permit you to damn. You will not sneak by with the rest of your lifespan. I have foreshortened the usual course of history and have let you discover the nature of the payment you had hoped to switch to the shoulders of others. It is the last of your own living power that will now be drained to provide the unearned for the worshippers and carriers of Death. Do not pretend that a malevolent reality defeated you—you were defeated by your own evasions. Do not pretend that you will perish for a noble ideal—you will perish as fodder for the haters of man.

"But to those of you who still retain a remnant of the dignity and will to love one's life, I am offering the chance to make a choice. Choose whether you wish to perish for a morality you have never believed or practiced. Pause on the brink of self-destruction and examine your values and your life. You had known how to take an inventory of your wealth. Now take an inventory of your mind.

"Since childhood, you have been hiding the guilty secret that you feel no desire to be moral, no desire to seek self-immolation, that you dread and hate your code, but dare not say it even to yourself, that you're devoid of those moral 'instincts' which others profess to feel. The less you felt, the louder you proclaimed your selfless love and servitude to others, in dread of ever letting them discover your own self, the self that you betrayed, the self that you kept in concealment, like a skeleton in the closet of your body. And they, who were at once your dupes and your deceivers, they listened and voiced their loud approval, in dread of ever letting you discover that they were harboring the same unspoken secret. Existence among you is a giant pretense, an act you all perform for one another, each feeling that he is the only guilty freak, each placing his moral authority in the unknowable known only to others, each faking the reality he feels they expect him to fake, none having the courage to break the vicious circle.

"No matter what dishonorable compromise you've made with your impracticable creed, no matter what miserable balance, half-cynicism, half-superstition, you now manage to maintain, you still preserve the root, the lethal tenet: the belief that the moral and the practical are opposites. Since childhood, you have been running from the terror of a choice you have never dared fully to identify: If the *practical*, whatever you must practice to exist, whatever works, succeeds, achieves your purpose, whatever brings you food and joy, whatever profits you, is evil—and if the good, the moral, is the *impractical*, whatever fails, destroys, frustrates, whatever injures you and brings you loss or pain—then your choice is to be moral or to live.

"The sole result of that murderous doctrine was to remove morality from life. You grew up to believe that moral laws bear no relation to the job of living, except as an impediment and threat, that man's existence is an amoral jungle where anything goes and anything works. And in that fog of switching definitions which descends upon a frozen mind, you have forgotten that the evils damned by your creed were the virtues required for living, and you have come to believe that actual evils are the *practical* means of existence. Forgetting that the impractical 'good' was self-sacrifice, you believe that self-esteem is impractical; forgetting that the practical 'evil' was production, you believe that robbery is practical.

"Swinging like a helpless branch in the wind of an uncharted moral wilderness, you dare not fully to be evil or fully to live. When you are honest, you feel the resentment of a sucker; when you cheat, you feel terror and shame. When you are happy, your joy is diluted by guilt; when you suffer, your pain is augmented by the feeling that pain is your natural state. You pity the men you admire, you believe they are doomed to fail; you envy the men you hate, you believe they are the masters of existence. You feel disarmed when you come up against a scoundrel: you believe that evil is bound to win, since the moral is the impotent, the *impractical*.

"Morality, to you, is a phantom scarecrow made of duty, of boredom, of punishment, of pain, a cross-breed between the first schoolteacher of your past and the tax collector of your present, a scarecrow standing in a barren field, waving a stick to chase away your pleasures—and *pleasure,* to you, is a liquor-soggy brain, a mindless slut, the stupor of a moron who stakes his cash on some animal's race, since pleasure cannot be moral.

"If you identify your actual belief, you will find a triple damnation—of yourself, of life, of virtue—in the grotesque conclusion you have reached: you believe that morality is a necessary evil.

"Do you wonder why you live without dignity, love without fire and die without resistance? Do you wonder why, wherever you look, you see nothing but unanswerable questions, why your life is torn by impossible conflicts, why you spend it straddling irrational fences to evade artificial choices, such as soul or body, mind or heart, security or freedom, private profit or public good?

"Do you cry that you find no answers? By what means did you hope to find them? You reject your tool of perception—your mind—then complain that the universe is a mystery. You discard your key, then wail that all doors are locked against you. You start out in pursuit of the irrational, then damn existence for making no sense.

"The fence you have been straddling for two hours—while hearing my words and seeking to escape them—is the coward's formula contained in the sentence: 'But we don't have to go to extremes!' The extreme you have always struggled to avoid is the recognition that reality is final, that A is A and that the truth is true. A moral code impossible to practice, a code that demands imperfection or death, has taught you to dissolve all ideas in fog, to permit no firm definitions, to regard any concept as approximate and any rule of conduct as elastic, to hedge on any principle, to compromise on any value, to take the middle of any road. By extorting your acceptance of supernatural absolutes, it has forced you to reject the absolute of nature. By making moral judgments impossible, it has made you incapable of rational judgment. A code that forbids you to cast the first stone, has forbidden you to admit the identity of stones and to know when or if you're being stoned.

"The man who refuses to judge, who neither agrees nor disagrees, who declares that there are no absolutes and believes that he escapes responsibility, is the man responsible for all the blood that is now spilled in the world. Reality is an absolute, existence is an absolute, a speck of dust is an absolute and so is a human life. Whether you live or die is an absolute. Whether you have a piece of bread or not, is an absolute. Whether you eat your bread or see it vanish into a looter's stomach, is an absolute.

"There are two sides to every issue: one side is right and the other is wrong, but the middle is always evil. The man who is wrong still retains some respect for truth, if only by accepting the responsibility of choice. But the man in the middle is the knave who blanks out the truth in order to pretend that no choice or values exist, who is willing to sit out the course of any battle, willing to cash in on the blood of the innocent or to crawl on his belly to the guilty, who dispenses justice by condemning both the robber and the robbed to jail, who solves conflicts by ordering the thinker and the fool to meet each other halfway. In any compromise between food and poison, it is only death that can win. In any compromise between good and evil, it is only evil that can profit. In that transfusion of blood which drains the good to feed the evil, the compromiser is the transmitting rubber tube.

"You, who are half-rational, half-coward, have been playing a con game with reality, but the victim you have conned is yourself. When men reduce their virtues to the approximate, then evil acquires the force of an absolute, when loyalty to an unyielding purpose is dropped by the virtuous, it's picked up by scoundrels—and you get the indecent spectacle of a cringing, bargaining, traitorous good and a self-righteously uncompromising evil. As you surrendered to the mystics of muscle when they told you that ignorance consists of claiming knowledge, so now you surrender to them when they shriek that immorality consists of pronouncing moral judgment. When they yell that it is selfish to be certain that you are right, you hasten to assure them that you're certain of nothing. When they shout that it's immoral to stand on your convictions, you assure them that you have no convictions whatever. When the thugs of Europe's People's States snarl that you are guilty of intolerance, because you don't treat your desire to

live and their desire to kill you as a difference of opinion—
you cringe and hasten to assure them that you are not in-
tolerant of any horror. When some barefoot bum in some
pesthole of Asia yells at you: How dare you be rich—you
apologize and beg him to be patient and promise him you'll
give it all away.

"You have reached the blind alley of the treason you committed when you agreed that you had no right to exist. Once,
you believed it was 'only a compromise': you conceded it
was evil to live for yourself, but moral to live for the sake of
your children. Then you conceded that it was selfish to live
for your children, but moral to live for your community.
Then you conceded that it was selfish to live for your community, but moral to live for your country. *Now*, you are letting this greatest of countries be devoured by any scum
from any corner of the earth, while you concede that it is
selfish to live for your country and that your moral duty is
to live for the globe. A man who has no right to life, has
no right to values and will not keep them.

"At the end of your road of successive betrayals, stripped
of weapons, of certainty, of honor, you commit your final act
of treason and sign your petition of intellectual bankruptcy:
while the muscle-mystics of the People's States proclaim that
they're the champions of reason and science, you agree and
hasten to proclaim that *faith* is your cardinal principle, that
reason is on the side of your destroyers, but yours is the side
of faith. To the struggling remnants of rational honesty in
the twisted, bewildered minds of your children, you declare
that you can offer no rational argument to support the ideas
that created this country, that there is no rational justification for freedom, for property, for justice, for rights, that they
rest on a mystical insight and can be accepted only on
faith, that in reason and logic the enemy is right, but faith
is superior to reason. You declare to your children that
it is rational to loot, to torture, to enslave, to expropriate,
to murder, but that they must resist the temptations of logic
and stick to the discipline of remaining irrational—that skyscrapers, factories, radios, airplanes were the products of
faith and mystic intuition, while famines, concentration camps
and firing squads are the products of a reasonable manner of
existence—that the industrial revolution was the revolt of the
men of faith against that era of reason and logic which is
known as the Middle Ages. Simultaneously, in the same breath,

to the same child, you declare that the looters who rule the People's States will surpass this country in material production, since they are the representatives of science, but that it's evil to be concerned with physical wealth and that one must renounce material prosperity—you declare that the looters' ideals are noble, but they do not mean them, while you do; that your purpose in fighting the looters is only to accomplish their aims, which they cannot accomplish, but you can; and that the way to fight them is to beat them to it and give one's wealth away. Then you wonder why your children join the People's thugs or become half-crazed delinquents, you wonder why the looters' conquests keep creeping closer to your doors—and you blame it on human stupidity, declaring that the masses are impervious to reason.

"You blank out the open, public spectacle of the looters' fight against the mind, and the fact that their bloodiest horrors are unleashed to punish the crime of thinking. You blank out the fact that most mystics of muscle started out as mystics of spirit, that they keep switching from one to the other, that the men you call materialists and spiritualists are only two halves of the same dissected human, forever seeking completion, but seeking it by swinging from the destruction of the flesh to the destruction of the soul and vice versa —that they keep running from your colleges to the slave pens of Europe to an open collapse into the mystic muck of India, seeking any refuge against reality, any form of escape from the mind.

"You blank it out and cling to your hypocrisy of 'faith' in order to blank out the knowledge that the looters have a stranglehold upon you, which consists of your moral code— that the looters are the final and consistent practitioners of the morality you're half-obeying, half-evading—that they practice it the only way it can be practiced: by turning the earth into a sacrificial furnace—that your morality forbids you to oppose them in the only way they can be opposed; by refusing to become a sacrificial animal and proudly asserting your right to exist—that in order to fight them to the finish and with full rectitude, *it is your morality that you have to reject.*

"You blank it out, because your self-esteem is tied to that mystic 'unselfishness' which you've never possessed or practiced, but spent so many years pretending to possess that the thought of denouncing it fills you with terror. No value is higher than self-esteem, but you've invested it in counterfeit securities—and now your morality has caught you in a trap where you are forced to protect your self-esteem by fighting for the creed of self-destruction. The grim joke is on you: that need of self-esteem, which you're unable to explain or to define, belongs to *my* morality, not yours; it's the objective token of my code, it is my proof within your own soul.

"By a feeling he has not learned to identify, but has derived from his first awareness of existence, from his discovery that he has to make choices, man knows that his desperate need of self-esteem is a matter of life or death. As a being of volitional consciousness, he knows that he must know his own value in order to maintain his own life. He knows that he has to be *right;* to be wrong in action means danger to his life; to be wrong in person, to be *evil,* means to be unfit for existence.

"Every act of man's life has to be willed; the mere act of obtaining or eating his food implies that the person he preserves is worthy of being preserved; every pleasure he seeks to enjoy implies that the person who seeks it is worthy of finding enjoyment. He has no choice about his need of self-esteem, his only choice is the standard by which to gauge it. And he makes his fatal error when he switches this gauge protecting his life into the service of his own destruction, when he chooses a standard contradicting existence and sets his self-esteem against reality.

"Every form of causeless self-doubt, every feeling of inferiority and secret unworthiness is, in fact, man's hidden dread of his inability to deal with existence. But the greater his terror, the more fiercely he clings to the murderous doctrines that choke him. No man can survive the moment of pronouncing himself irredeemably evil; should he do it, his next moment is insanity or suicide. To escape it—if he's chosen an irrational standard—he will fake, evade, blank out; he will cheat himself of reality, of existence, of happiness, of mind; and he will ultimately cheat himself of self-esteem by struggling to preserve its illusion rather than to risk discovering its lack. To fear to face an issue is to believe that the worst is true.

"It is not any crime you have ever committed that infects your soul with permanent guilt, it is none of your failures, errors or flaws, but the *blank-out* by which you attempt to evade them—it is not any sort of Original Sin or unknown prenatal deficiency, but the knowledge and fact of your basic default, of suspending your mind, of refusing to think. Fear and guilt are your chronic emotions, they are real and you do deserve them, but they don't come from the superficial reasons you invent to disguise their cause, not from your 'selfishness,' weakness or ignorance, but from a real and basic threat to your existence: *fear*, because you have abandoned your weapon of survival, *guilt*, because you know you have done it volitionally.

"The *self* you have betrayed is your mind; *self-esteem* is reliance on one's power to think. The ego you seek, that essential '*you*' which you cannot express or define, is not your emotions or inarticulate dreams, but your *intellect*, that judge of your supreme tribunal whom you've impeached in order to drift at the mercy of any stray shyster you describe as your 'feeling.' Then you drag yourself through a self-made night, in a desperate quest for a nameless fire, moved by some fading vision of a dawn you had seen and lost.

"Observe the persistence, in mankind's mythologies, of the legend about a paradise that men had once possessed, the city of Atlantis or the Garden of Eden or some kingdom of perfection, always behind us. The root of that legend exists, not in the past of the race, but in the past of every man. You still retain a sense—not as firm as a memory, but diffused like the pain of hopeless longing—that somewhere in the starting years of your childhood, before you had learned to submit, to absorb the terror of unreason and to doubt the value of your mind, you had known a radiant state of existence, you had known the independence of a rational consciousness facing an open universe. *That* is the paradise which you have lost, which you seek—which is yours for the taking.

"Some of you will never know who is John Galt. But those of you who have known a single moment of love for existence and of pride in being its worthy lover, a moment of looking at this earth and letting your glance be its sanction, have known the state of being a man, and I—I am only the man who knew that that state is not to be betrayed. I am the man who knew what made it possible and who chose consistently to practice and to be what you had practiced and been in that one moment.

"That choice is yours to make. That choice—the dedication to one's highest potential—is made by accepting the fact that the noblest act you have ever performed is the act of your mind in the process of grasping that two and two make four.

"Whoever you are—you who are alone with my words in this moment, with nothing but your honesty to help you understand—the choice is still open to be a human being, but the price is to start from scratch, to stand naked in the face of reality and, reversing a costly historical error, to declare: 'I am, therefore I'll think.'

"Accept the irrevocable fact that your life depends upon your mind. Admit that the whole of your struggle, your doubts, your fakes, your evasions, was a desperate quest for escape from the responsibility of a volitional consciousness—a quest for automatic knowledge, for instinctive action, for intuitive certainty—and while you called it a longing for the state of an angel, what you were seeking was the state of an animal. Accept, as your moral ideal, the task of becoming a man.

"Do not say that you're afraid to trust your mind because you know so little. Are you safer in surrendering to mystics and discarding the little that you know? Live and act within the limit of your knowledge and keep expanding it to the limit of your life. Redeem your mind from the hockshops of authority. Accept the fact that you are not omniscient, but playing a zombie will not give you omniscience—that your mind is fallible, but becoming mindless will not make you infallible—that an error made on your own is safer than ten truths accepted on faith, because the first leaves you the means to correct it, but the second destroys your capacity to distinguish truth from error. In place of your dream of an omniscient automaton, accept the fact that any knowledge man acquires is acquired by his own will and effort, and that *that* is his distinction in the universe, *that* is his nature, his morality, his glory.

"Discard that unlimited license to evil which consists of claiming that man is imperfect. By what standard do you damn him when you claim it? Accept the fact that in the realm of morality nothing less than perfection will do. But perfection is not to be gauged by mystic commandments to practice the impossible, and your moral stature is not to be gauged by matters not open to your choice. Man has a single basic choice: to think or not, and *that* is the gauge of his virtue. Moral perfection is an *unbreached rationality*—not the degree of your intelligence, but the full and relentless use of your mind, not the extent of your knowledge, but the acceptance of reason as an absolute.

"Learn to distinguish the difference between errors of knowledge and breaches of morality. An error of knowledge is not a moral flaw, provided you are willing to correct it; only a mystic would judge human beings by the standard of an impossible, automatic omniscience. But a breach of morality is the conscious choice of an action you know to be evil, or a willful evasion of knowledge, a suspension of sight and of thought. That which you do not know, is not a moral charge against you; but that which you refuse to know, is an account of infamy growing in your soul. Make every allowance for errors of knowledge; do not forgive or accept any breach of morality. Give the benefit of the doubt to those who seek to know; but treat as potential killers those specimens of insolent depravity who make demands upon you, announcing that they have and seek no reasons, proclaiming, as a license, that they 'just feel it'—or those who reject an irrefutable argument by saying: 'It's only logic,' which means: 'It's only reality.' The only realm opposed to reality is the realm and premise of death.

"Accept the fact that the achievement of your happiness is the only *moral* purpose of your life, and that *happiness*—not pain or mindless self-indulgence—is the proof of your moral integrity, since it is the proof and the result of your loyalty to the achievement of your values. Happiness was the responsibility you dreaded, it required the kind of rational discipline you did not value yourself enough to assume—and the anxious staleness of your days is the monument to your evasion of the knowledge that there is no moral substitute for happiness, that there is no more despicable coward than the man who deserted the battle for his joy, fearing to assert his right to existence, lacking the courage and the loyalty to life of a bird or a flower reaching for the sun. Discard the protective rags of that vice which you call a virtue: humility—learn to value yourself, which means: to fight for your happiness—and when you learn that *pride* is the sum of all virtues, you will learn to live like a man.

"As a basic step of self-esteem, learn to treat as the mark of a cannibal any man's *demand* for your help. To demand it is to claim that your life is *his* property—and loathsome as such claim might be, there's something still more loathsome: your agreement. Do you ask if it's ever proper to help another man? No—if he claims it as his right or as a moral duty that you owe him. Yes—if such is your own desire based on your own selfish pleasure in the value of his person and his struggle. Suffering as such is not a value; only man's fight against suffering, is. If you choose to help a man who suffers, do it only on the ground of his virtues, of his fight to recover, of his rational record, or of the fact that he suffers unjustly; then your action is still a trade, and his virtue is the payment for your help. But to help a man who has no virtues, to help him on the ground of his suffering as such, to accept his faults, his *need*, as a claim— is to accept the mortgage of a zero on your values. A man who has no virtues is a hater of existence who acts on the premise of death; to help him is to sanction his evil and to support his career of destruction. Be it only a penny you will not miss or a kindly smile he has not earned, a tribute to a zero is treason to life and to all those who struggle to maintain it. It is of such pennies and smiles that the desolation of your world was made.

"Do not say that my morality is too hard for you to practice and that you fear it as you fear the unknown. Whatever living moments you have known, were lived by the values of *my* code. But you stifled, negated, betrayed it. You kept sacrificing your virtues to your vices, and the best among men to the worst. Look around you: what you have done to society, you had done it first within your soul; one is the image of the other. This dismal wreckage, which is now your world, is the physical form of the treason you committed to your values, to your friends, to your defenders, to your future, to your country, to yourself.

"We—whom you are now calling, but who will not answer any longer—we had lived among you, but you failed to know us, you refused to think and to see what we were. You failed to recognize the motor I invented—and it became, in *your* world, a pile of dead scrap. You failed to recognize the hero in your soul—and you failed to know me when I passed you in the street. When you cried in despair for the unattainable spirit which you felt had deserted your world, you gave it my name, but what you were calling was your own betrayed self-esteem. You will not recover one without the other.

"When you failed to give recognition to man's mind and

attempted to rule human beings by force—those who sub-mitted had no mind to surrender; those who had, were men who don't submit. Thus the man of productive genius as-sumed in *your* world the disguise of a playboy and became a destroyer of wealth, choosing to annihilate his fortune rather than surrender it to guns. Thus the thinker, the man of reason, assumed in *your* world the role of a pirate, to defend his values by force against your force, rather than submit to the rule of brutality. Do you hear me, Francisco d'Anconia and Ragnar Danneskjöld, my first friends, my fel-low fighters, my fellow outcasts, in whose name and honor I speak?

"It was the three of us who started what I am now completing. It was the three of us who resolved to avenge this country and to release its imprisoned soul. This greatest of countries was built on *my* morality—on the inviolate supremacy of man's right to exist—but you dreaded to admit it and live up to it. You stared at an achievement unequaled in history, you looted its effects and blanked out its cause. In the presence of that monument to human morality, which is a factory, a highway or a bridge—you kept damning this country as immoral and its progress as 'material greed,' you kept offering apologies for this country's greatness to the idol of primordial starvation, to decaying Europe's idol of a leprous, mystic bum.

"This country—the product of *reason*—could not survive on the morality of sacrifice. It was not built by men who sought self-immolation or by men who sought handouts. It could not stand on the mystic split that divorced man's soul from his body. It could not live by the mystic doctrine that damned this earth as evil and those who succeeded on earth as depraved. From its start, this country was a threat to the ancient rule of mystics. In the brilliant rocket-explosion of its youth, this country displayed to an incredulous world what greatness was possible to man, what happiness was possible on earth. It was one or the other: America or mys-tics. The mystics knew it; you didn't. You let them infect you with the worship of *need*—and this country became a giant in body with a mooching midget in place of its soul, while its living soul was driven underground to labor and feed you in silence, unnamed, unhonored, negated, its soul and hero: the industrialist. Do you hear me now, Hank Rearden, the greatest of the victims I have avenged?

"Neither he nor the rest of us will return until the road is clear to rebuild this country—until the wreckage of the morality of sacrifice has been wiped out of our way. A country's political system is based on its code of morality. We will rebuild America's system on the moral premise which had been its foundation, but which you treated as a guilty underground, in your frantic evasion of the conflict between that premise and your mystic morality: the premise that man is an end in himself, not the means to the ends of others, that man's life, his freedom, his happiness are *his* by inalienable right.

"You who've lost the concept of a right, you who swing in impotent evasiveness between the claim that rights are a gift of God, a supernatural gift to be taken on faith, or the claim that rights are a gift of society, to be broken at its arbitrary whim—the source of man's rights is not divine law or congressional law, but the law of identity. A is A—and Man is Man. *Rights* are conditions of existence required by man's nature for his proper survival. If man is to live on earth, it is *right* for him to use his mind, it is *right* to act on his own free judgment, it is *right* to work for his values and to keep the product of his work. If life on earth is his purpose, he has a *right* to live as a rational being: nature forbids him the irrational. Any group, any gang, any nation that attempts to negate man's rights, is *wrong*, which means: is evil, which means: is anti-life.

"*Rights* are a moral concept—and morality is a matter of choice. Men are free not to choose man's survival as the standard of their morals and their laws, but not free to escape from the fact that the alternative is a cannibal society, which exists for a while by devouring its best and collapses like a cancerous body, when the healthy have been eaten by the diseased, when the rational have been consumed by the irrational. Such has been the fate of your societies in history, but you've evaded the knowledge of the cause. I am here to state it: the agent of retribution was the law of identity, which you cannot escape. Just as man cannot live by means of the irrational, so two men cannot, or two thousand, or two billion. Just as man can't succeed by defying reality, so a nation can't, or a country, or a globe. A is A. The rest is a matter of time, provided by the generosity of victims.

"Just as man can't exist without his body, so no rights

can exist without the right to translate one's rights into reality—to think, to work and to keep the results—which means: the right of property. The modern mystics of muscle who offer you the fraudulent alternative of 'human rights' versus 'property rights,' as if one could exist without the other, are making a last, grotesque attempt to revive the doctrine of soul versus body. Only a ghost can exist without material property; only a slave can work with no right to the product of his effort. The doctrine that 'human rights' are superior to 'property rights' simply means that some human beings have the right to make property out of others; since the competent have nothing to gain from the incompetent, it means the right of the incompetent to own their betters and to use them as productive cattle. Whoever regards this as human and right, has no right to the title of 'human.'

"The source of property rights is the law of causality. All property and all forms of wealth are produced by man's mind and labor. As you cannot have effects without causes, so you cannot have wealth without its source: without intelligence. You cannot force intelligence to work: those who're able to think, will not work under compulsion; those who will, won't produce much more than the price of the whip needed to keep them enslaved. You cannot obtain the products of a mind except on the owner's terms, by trade and by volitional consent. Any other policy of men toward man's property is the policy of criminals, no matter what their numbers. Criminals are savages who play it short-range and starve when their prey runs out—just as you're starving today, you who believed that crime could be 'practical' if your government decreed that robbery was legal and resistance to robbery illegal.

"The only proper purpose of a government is to protect man's rights, which means: to protect him from physical violence. A proper government is only a policeman, acting as an agent of man's self-defense, and, as such, may resort to force *only* against those who *start* the use of force. The only proper functions of a government are: the police, to protect you from criminals; the army, to protect you from foreign invaders; and the courts, to protect your property and contracts from breach or fraud by others, to settle disputes by rational rules, according to *objective* law. But a government that *initiates* the employment of force against men who had forced no one, the employment of armed compulsion against disarmed victims, is a nightmare infernal machine designed to annihilate morality: such a government reverses its only moral purpose and switches from the role of protector to the role of man's deadliest enemy, from the role of policeman to the role of a criminal vested with the right to the wielding of violence against victims deprived of the right of self-defense. Such a government substitutes for morality the following rule of social conduct: you may do whatever you please to your neighbor, provided your gang is bigger than his.

"Only a brute, a fool or an evader can agree to exist on such terms or agree to give his fellow men a blank check on his life and his mind, to accept the belief that others have the right to dispose of his person at their whim, that the will of the majority is omnipotent, that the physical force of muscles and numbers is a substitute for justice, reality and truth. We, the men of the mind, we who are traders, not masters or slaves, do not deal in blank checks or grant them. We do not live or work with any form of the non-objective.

"So long as men, in the era of savagery, had no concept of objective reality and believed that physical nature was ruled by the whim of unknowable demons—no thought, no science, no production were possible. Only when men discovered that nature was a firm, predictable absolute were they able to rely on their knowledge, to choose their course, to plan their future and, slowly, to rise from the cave. *Now* you have placed modern industry, with its immense complexity of scientific precision, back into the power of unknowable demons—the unpredictable power of the arbitrary whims of hidden, ugly little bureaucrats. A farmer will not invest the effort of one summer if he's unable to calculate his chances of a harvest. But you expect industrial giants—who plan in terms of decades, invest in terms of generations and undertake ninety-nine-year contracts—to continue to function and produce, not knowing what random caprice in the skull of what random official will descend upon them at what moment to demolish the whole of their effort. Drifters and physical laborers live and plan by the range of a day. The better the mind, the longer the range. A man whose vision extends to a shanty, might continue to build on your quicksands, to grab a fast profit and run. A man who envisions skyscrapers, will not. Nor will he give ten years of unswerving devotion to the task of inventing a new product, when he knows that gangs of entrenched mediocrity are juggling the laws against him, to tie him, restrict him and force him to fail, but should he fight them and struggle and succeed, they will seize his rewards and his invention.

"Look past the range of the moment, you who cry that you fear to compete with men of superior intelligence, that their mind is a threat to your livelihood, that the strong leave no chance to the weak in a market of voluntary trade. What determines the material value of your work? Nothing but the productive effort of your mind—if you lived on a desert island. The less efficient the thinking of your brain, the less your physical labor would bring you—and you could spend your life on a single routine, collecting a precarious harvest or hunting with bow and arrows, unable to think any further. But when you live in a rational society, where men are free to trade, you receive an incalculable bonus: the material value of your work is determined not only by your effort, but by the effort of the best productive minds who exist in the world around you.

"When you work in a modern factory, you are paid, not only for your labor, but for all the productive genius which has made that factory possible: for the work of the industrialist who built it, for the work of the investor who saved the money to risk on the untried and the new, for the work of the engineer who designed the machines of which you are pushing the levers, for the work of the inventor who created the product which you spend your time on making, for the work of the scientist who discovered the laws that went into the making of that product, for the work of the philosopher who taught men how to think and whom you spend your time denouncing.

"The machine, the frozen form of a living intelligence, is the power that expands the potential of your life by raising the productivity of your time. If you worked as a blacksmith in the mystics' Middle Ages, the whole of your earning capacity would consist of an iron bar produced by your hands in days and days of effort. How many tons of rail do you produce per day if you work for Hank Rearden? Would you dare to claim that the size of your pay check was created solely by your physical labor and that those rails were the product of your muscles? The standard of living of that blacksmith is all that your muscles are worth; the rest is a gift from Hank Rearden.

"Every man is free to rise as far as he's able or willing, but it's only the degree to which he thinks that determines the degree to which he'll rise. Physical labor as such can extend no further than the range of the moment. The man who does no more than physical labor, consumes the material value-equivalent of his own contribution to the process of production, and leaves no further value, neither for himself nor others. But the man who produces an idea in any field of rational endeavor—the man who discovers new knowledge —is the permanent benefactor of humanity. Material products can't be shared, they belong to some ultimate consumer; it is only the value of an idea that can be shared with unlimited numbers of men, making all sharers richer at no one's sacrifice or loss, raising the productive capacity of whatever labor they perform. It is the value of his own time that the strong of the intellect transfers to the weak, letting them work on the jobs he discovered, while devoting his time to further discoveries. This is mutual trade to mutual advantage; the interests of the mind are one, no matter what the degree of intelligence, among men who desire to work and don't seek or expect the unearned.

"In proportion to the mental energy he spent, the man who creates a new invention receives but a small percentage of his value in terms of material payment, no matter what fortune he makes, no matter what millions he earns. But the man who works as a janitor in the factory producing that invention, receives an enormous payment in proportion to the mental effort that his job requires of *him*. And the same is true of all men between, on all levels of ambition and ability. The man at the top of the intellectual pyramid contributes the most of all those below him, but gets nothing except his material payment, receiving no intellectual bonus from others to add to the value of his time. The man at the bottom who, left to himself, would starve in his hopeless ineptitude, contributes nothing to those above him, but receives the bonus of all of their brains. Such is the nature of the 'competition' between the strong and the weak of the intellect. Such is the pattern of 'exploitation' for which you have damned the strong.

"Such was the service we had given you and were glad and willing to give. What did we ask in return? Nothing but freedom. We required that you leave us free to function—free to think and to work as we choose—free to take our own risks and to bear our own losses—free to earn our own profits and to make our own fortunes—free to gamble on *your* rationality, to submit our products to your judgment for the purpose of a voluntary trade, to rely on the objective value of our work and on your mind's ability to see it—free to count on your intelligence and honesty, and to deal with nothing but your mind. Such was the price we asked, which you chose to reject as too high. You decided to call it unfair that we, who had dragged you out of your hovels and provided you with modern apartments, with radios, movies and cars, should own our palaces and yachts—you decided that *you* had a right to your wages, but *we* had no right to our profits, that you did not want us to deal with your mind, but to deal, instead, with your gun. Our answer to *that*, was: 'May you be damned!' Our answer came true. You are.

"You did not care to compete in terms of intelligence—you are now competing in terms of brutality. You did not care to allow rewards to be won by successful production—you are now running a race in which rewards are won by successful plunder. You called it selfish and cruel that men should trade value for value—you have now established an unselfish society where they trade extortion for extortion. Your system is a legal civil war, where men gang up on one another and struggle for possession of the law, which they use as a club over rivals, till another gang wrests it from their clutch and clubs them with it in their turn, all of them clamoring protestations of service to an unnamed public's unspecified good. You had said that you saw no difference between economic and political power, between the power of money and the power of guns—no difference between reward and punishment, no difference between purchase and plunder, no difference between pleasure and fear, no difference between life and death. You are learning the difference now.

"Some of you might plead the excuse of your ignorance, of a limited mind and a limited range. But the damned and the guiltiest among you are the men who *had* the capacity to know, yet chose to blank out reality, the men who were willing to sell their intelligence into cynical servitude to force: the contemptible breed of those mystics of science who profess a devotion to some sort of 'pure knowledge'—the purity consisting of their claim that such knowledge has no practical purpose on this earth—who reserve their logic for inanimate matter, but believe that the subject of dealing with men requires and deserves no rationality, who scorn money and sell their souls in exchange for a laboratory supplied by loot. And since there is no such thing as 'non-practical knowledge' or any sort of 'disinterested' action, since they scorn the use of their science for the purpose and profit of life, they deliver their science to the service of death, to the only practical purpose it can ever have for looters: to inventing weapons of coercion and destruction. They, the intellects who seek escape from moral values, *they* are the damned on this earth, *theirs* is the guilt beyond forgiveness. Do you hear me, Dr. Robert Stadler?

"But it is not to him that I wish to speak. I am speaking to those among you who have retained some sovereign shred of their soul, unsold and unstamped: '—to the order of others.' If, in the chaos of the motives that have made you listen to the radio tonight, there was an honest, *rational* desire to learn what is wrong with the world, you are the man whom I wished to address. By the rules and terms of my code, one owes a rational statement to those whom it does concern and who're making an effort to know. Those who're making an effort to fail to understand me, are not a concern of mine.

"I am speaking to those who desire to live and to recapture the honor of their soul. Now that you know the truth about your world, *stop supporting your own destroyers.* The evil of the world is made possible by nothing but the sanction you give it. Withdraw your sanction. Withdraw your support. Do not try to live on your enemies' terms or to win at a game where they're setting the rules. Do not seek the favor of those who enslaved you, do not beg for alms from those who have robbed you, be it subsidies, loans or jobs, do not join their team to recoup what they've taken by helping them rob your neighbors. One cannot pay to maintain one's life by accepting bribes to condone one's destruction. Do not struggle for profit, success or security at the price of a lien on your right to exist. Such a lien is not to be paid off; the more you pay them, the more they will demand; the greater the values you seek or achieve, the more vulnerably helpless you become. Theirs is a system of *white blackmail* devised to bleed you, not by means of your sins, but by means of your love for existence.

"Do not attempt to rise on the looters' terms or to climb a ladder while they're holding the ropes. Do not allow their hands to touch the only power that keeps them in power: your living ambition. Go on strike—in the manner I did. Use your mind and skill in private, extend your knowledge, develop your ability, but do not share your achievements with others. Do not try to produce a fortune, with a looter riding on your back. Stay on the lowest rung of their ladder, earn no more than your barest survival, do not make an extra penny to support the looters' state. Since you're captive, act as a captive, do not help them pretend that you're free. Be the silent, incorruptible enemy they dread. When they force you, obey—but *do not volunteer*. Never volunteer a step in their direction, or a wish, or a plea, or a purpose. Do not help a holdup man to claim that he acts as your friend and benefactor. Do not help your jailers to pretend that their jail is your natural state of existence. Do not help them to fake reality. That fake is the only dam holding off their secret terror, the terror of knowing they're unfit to exist; remove it and let them drown; your sanction is their only life belt.

"If you find a chance to vanish into some wilderness out of their reach, do so, but not to exist as a bandit or to create a gang competing with their racket; build a productive life of your own with those who accept your moral code and are willing to struggle for a human existence. You have no chance to win on the Morality of Death or by the code of faith and force; raise a standard to which the honest *will* repair: the standard of Life and Reason.

"Act as a rational being and aim at becoming a rallying point for all those who are starved for a voice of integrity— act on your rational values, whether alone in the midst of your enemies, or with a few of your chosen friends, or as the founder of a modest community on the frontier of mankind's rebirth.

"When the looters' state collapses, deprived of the best of its slaves, when it falls to a level of impotent chaos, like the mystic-ridden nations of the Orient, and dissolves into starving robber gangs fighting to rob one another—when the advocates of the morality of sacrifice perish with their final ideal—then and on that day we will return.

"We will open the gates of our city to those who deserve to enter, a city of smokestacks, pipe lines, orchards, markets and inviolate homes. We will act as the rallying center for such hidden outposts as you'll build. With the sign of the dollar as our symbol—the sign of free trade and free minds —we will move to reclaim this country once more from the impotent savages who never discovered its nature, its meaning, its splendor. Those who choose to join us, will join us; those who don't, will not have the power to stop us; hordes of savages have never been an obstacle to men who carried the banner of the mind.

"Then this country will once more become a sanctuary for a vanishing species: the rational being. The political system we will build is contained in a single moral premise: no man may obtain any values from others by resorting to physical force. Every man will stand or fall, live or die by his rational judgment. If he fails to use it and falls, he will be his only victim. If he fears that his judgment is inadequate, he will not be given a gun to improve it. If he chooses to correct his errors in time, he will have the unobstructed example of his betters, for guidance in learning to think; but an end will be put to the infamy of paying with one life for the errors of another.

"In that world, you'll be able to rise in the morning with the spirit you had known in your childhood: that spirit of eagerness, adventure and certainty which comes from dealing with a rational universe. No child is afraid of nature; it is your fear of men that will vanish, the fear that has stunted your soul, the fear you acquired in your early encounters with the incomprehensible, the unpredictable, the contradictory, the arbitrary, the hidden, the faked, *the irrational* in men. You will live in a world of responsible beings, who will be as consistent and reliable as facts; the guarantee of their character will be a system of existence where objective reality is the standard and the judge. Your virtues will be given protection, your vices and weaknesses will not. Every chance will be open to your good, none will be provided for your evil. What you'll receive from men will not be alms, or pity, or mercy, or forgiveness of sins, but a single value: *justice*. And when you'll look at men or at yourself, you will feel, not disgust, suspicion and guilt, but a single constant: *respect*.

"Such is the future you are capable of winning. It requires a struggle; so does any human value. All life is a purposeful struggle and your only choice is the choice of a goal. Do you wish to continue the battle of your present or do you wish to fight for my world? Do you wish to continue a struggle that consists of clinging to precarious ledges in a sliding descent to the abyss, a struggle where the hardships you endure are irreversible and the victories you win bring you closer to destruction? Or do you wish to undertake a struggle that consists of rising from ledge to ledge in a steady ascent to the top, a struggle where the hardships are investments in your future, and the victories bring you irreversibly closer to the world of your moral ideal, and should you die without reaching full sunlight, you will die on a level touched by its rays? Such is the choice before you. Let your mind and your love of existence decide.

"The last of my words will be addressed to those heroes who might still be hidden in the world, those who are held prisoner, not by their evasions, but by their virtues and their desperate courage. My brothers in spirit, check on your virtues and on the nature of the enemies you're serving. Your destroyers hold you by means of your endurance, your generosity, your innocence, your love—the endurance that carries their burdens—the generosity that responds to their cries of despair—the innocence that is unable to conceive of their evil and gives them the benefit of every doubt, refusing to condemn them without understanding and incapable of understanding such motives as theirs—the love, your love of life, which makes you believe that they are men and that they love it, too. But the world of today is the world they wanted; life is the object of their hatred. Leave them to the death they worship. In the name of your magnificent devotion to this earth, leave them, don't exhaust the greatness of your soul on achieving the triumph of the evil of theirs. Do you hear me . . . my love?

"In the name of the best within you, do not sacrifice this world to those who are its worst. In the name of the values that keep you alive, do not let your vision of man be distorted by the ugly, the cowardly, the mindless in those who have never achieved his title. Do not lose your knowledge that man's proper estate is an upright posture, an intransigent mind and a step that travels unlimited roads. Do not let your fire go out, spark by irreplaceable spark, in the hopeless swamps of the approximate, the not-quite, the not-yet, the not-at-all. Do not let the hero in your soul perish, in lonely frustration for the life you deserved, but have never been able to reach. Check your road and the nature of your battle. The world you desired can be won, it exists, it is real, it is possible, it's yours.

"But to win it requires your total dedication and a total break with the world of your past, with the doctrine that man is a sacrificial animal who exists for the pleasure of others. Fight for the value of your person. Fight for the virtue of your pride. Fight for the essence of that which is man: for his sovereign rational mind. Fight with the radiant certainty and the absolute rectitude of knowing that yours is the Morality of Life and that yours is the battle for any achievement, any value, any grandeur, any goodness, any joy that has ever existed on this earth.

"You will win when you are ready to pronounce the oath I have taken at the start of my battle—and for those who wish to know the day of my return, I shall now repeat it to the hearing of the world:

"I swear—by my life and my love of it—that I will never live for the sake of another man, nor ask another man to live for mine."